Somebody's Grandfather

Somebody's Grandfather

Nicole Watt

Somebody's Grandfather
Copyright © 2020 by Nicole Watt

All rights reserved. No part of this book may be used or reproduced in any manner whatsoever including Internet usage, without written permission of the author.

Book design by Maureen Cutajar
www.gopublished.com

ISBN-13: 978-1-7 16-49240-2

For Iwona,
The best walking partner anyone could ask for

Dear Reader,

Thank you for joining me on this journey.

Many of the people in this little book are strangers to me. Others I only knew for a short while. A few have become lifelong friends. Sometimes, there are no names to go with the faces. Other times, names have been changed or created to protect their identities or because I was unable to locate the person. Some details have been changed when necessary.

Among the ten stories, some of the people you will meet are a prostitute, a prison inmate, a woman with a disability, and homeless men. You will also meet the dedicated leader of a unique music band, and a woman with a special knack for helping others feel beautiful. Each one shining a light in some distinct way.

The way God sees people can be strikingly different than our human perspective. Through writing this book I have been deeply moved by the tenacity, integrity, and transcendent beauty of each person. Some I encountered in hard situations. Others had to overcome many hurdles in this human race we call life. A few have inspired me with their ability to draw out the best in others.

May you be blessed in reading these stories. May you see yourself somewhere in these pages. Now, perhaps more than ever, we need to see ourselves and each other the way God does. We are all His Somebody.

Love,
Nicole Watt
Northern Ireland 2020

Acknowledgments

Every book, even a little one like this, requires loads of help and expertise.

Thank you to my niece, Elizabeth Mann, for the cover photo.

To our cover models, Paul and Sarah.

To Denise Lālahi, for your incredible editing on many of these stories. You are a wise woman, a true treasure.

To Kaelin Ball, also for your insights and editing, not only of my words, but into my heart. Without heart, words do not matter.

And to the many friends who read and re-read copies, for your help and encouragement. I think I owe a few of you some new reading glasses.

To HS, for helping me see a little bit more the way heaven does.

Contents

Prophet 1

Somebody's Grandfather 7

Lily 13

Hero or Criminal 25

The Perfect Gift 31

Eye of the Beholder 37

Just Like You and Me 43

The Music Man 55

The Village Beauty 61

Into the Night 67

"You have never talked to a mere mortal."
– C.S. Lewis

Prophet

"Close those doors" he muttered as he stood on the subway platform, his rich chocolate brown face full of vexation and purpose. He wore a worn leather jacket and black turtleneck, a pair of ripped green shorts and flip flops though it was the middle of winter.

"*Close* those doors! Close *THOSE* doors! *CLOSE THOSE DOORS!*" With each emphasis his voice rose by increments until he was shouting. His head twisted frantically as he searched up and down the platform looking for someone who would listen to him and close the doors of the subway cars. His unanswered agitation was sad and frightening.

The repetitive opening and closing motions were common occurrence to us subway riders. Whether late comers were pushing their way aboard, or electrical switches were being tripped, trains rarely pulled out of the station until doors had opened and shut numerous times. It was nothing to be concerned about. Yet, this man was profoundly upset.

Passengers sat patiently on shiny orange seats in the yellow interior of the train, reading newspapers or listening to music. Some were so tired they had fallen asleep. Others stood, holding onto the gleaming handrails which hung from the roof, while staring at images seen only in their minds. Most barely noticed the young man and his earnest pleas for the doors to be closed. Homeless people with mental health issues could be commonplace in the underground subway areas, especially in winter. I did not know for certain that he was homeless but guessing by his clothes and unkempt appearance he probably was.

"Don't worry about him" the man next to me scoffed. "He's probably one of the crazies let loose when politicians had all the nuthouses shut down years ago." He scratched his unshaven face as he laughed and went back to reading his paper.

Being a newcomer to New York City from the Bald Hills of Pennsylvania, I was unfamiliar with this level of homelessness. This man was not the first person I had seen in such a poor state. The wild despair of it was haunting: the co-mingling of the haves and have-nots. Broken lives on public display. Even the most private acts exposed to so many unseeing eyes. The smell that made the eyes smart wafting from clothes unwashed for months, maybe years, begging next to those wearing Armani suits. Bodies wandering in the elements without a basic pair of shoes passed by women wearing diamond jewelry worth more than what I would pay in five years of rent.

"Would someone *close* these doors!" He groaned in agony. "Would someone put some *clothes* on these doors!"

He paused and repeated. "WOULD SOMEONE PLEASE PUT SOME CLOTHES ON THESE DOORS!"

Something cracked in the atmosphere between us as if he were suddenly alone on a stage, and I his only audience. He was right in front of me now, still on the platform but standing as close as he could to the subway doors directly across from my seat. A menacing look crossed his face. My heart thumped with fear and a chill passed through me though the car was warm from the forced heat. But fear soon melted into heartache as his face contorted in anguish.

"Someone *please* put some clothes on these doors!" He looked right at me, his voice raspy, spent.

Taking a deep breath, he seemed to gain a second wind. He shouted, his cries mounting in despair now.

"COVER THESE DOORS! THEY'RE NAKED! COVER THEM!"

I noticed afresh his bare legs, scraped, bruised and chalk-like from the cold, his feet cracked and blue, subjected to the elements in his broken flip flops. His dreads flopped loose and haggard around his face. Just as the next shrill call echoed from his veined throat, the doors closed, and the subway crept into the dark tunnel below the city toward the open air of Brooklyn. I broke out in a sweat, my heart thumping with relief. My last glimpse of him he was dancing on the platform.

My acting teacher had told us every life has its personal expression of universal truth, its voice a ripple in the collective waters. In the days that followed, I thought of that one man standing alone on the subway platform, and his progression from closing subway doors to pleading for someone to put clothes on the doors. I knew in my heart he was more than a ranting mad man, but I could not decipher the message. And then suddenly an impression came to me:

What if he was crying out the secret fear, the deep need of humankind: *We are all exposed. We are naked and vulnerable. Someone cover us.*

Moving from a rural community to a large metropolis had thrown me into a tailspin. All around me people seemed to have it together. Expensive cars, designer clothes and stoic faces were everywhere. Fancy coffees were sipped at sidewalk cafes, long layers of ivy spilled from terrace boxes, and flowers unfurled in front immaculate brownstones. And yet, often I met people who were lonely. They told me about the jobs they worked in, and hated but made them look and feel important, while dreaming of a different life. I'm sure there were people in similar situations back home. Perhaps living in such proximity with each other here just made it clearer.

Shy, yet overly expressive, with a wardrobe that was behind the times, I was regularly overlooked and underestimated. I wandered the maze of city streets looking for work, belonging, for some comfort from the new and overwhelming fears of being so far from home. I often felt exposed and alone. I thought I had come to the city with a sincere and humble desire to learn acting, but sometimes entertained fantasies about becoming famous, believing that would somehow make me feel better. Were these all just false coverings that were really no cover at all?

Was the man in the subway mentally ill, or could he truly been trying to tell us a universal truth? The Bible recounts many stories of God using prostitutes, poor uneducated fisherman - even a donkey - to announce His messages, and often no one listened. So, why not a homeless man in a city of millions? His words, spoken not from a shiny platform, but from his own deprived condition, lent him a credibility that gave me pause to wonder. But how could we cover ourselves? First, it would be necessary to lay down the facade. Wasn't that exactly what I was learning in acting class?

As I reflected on it all I believed that not only was God showing me my own need for Him, He was showing me how He sees His creations - homeless and uncovered here on this strange and beautiful earth, trying to protect ourselves with what can never satisfy, what can never meet our true need for love and belonging. Though I did not understand the full meaning of the message, it seemed to hold true that when I focused on all the good things I had like a warm apartment, food to eat, an act of kindness, a stranger's smile, sharing the truth of my feelings and experiences, the sensation of being covered, held even, was most evident. When I tried to hide behind the right haircut or outfit or say and do what others expected of me rather than be who I truly was, I felt even more vulnerable and alone. Though it was a lot for my young head to conceive, a glimmer of recognition emerged.

That cold winter day, with the stark bare trees pointing to the gray sky, a road was opened before me through the words of a messenger in the guise of a homeless man. He wandered in underground city streets and platforms, living in abandoned tunnels, afflicted for our sakes, with few listeners, yet still standing his holy ground.

Somebody's Grandfather

*S*unday Brunch was always hectic in New York City, and I had just started working at a restaurant where the standards were particularly high. Living contentedly in the gritty Lower East Side, I felt out of sync in the chic West Village restaurant with its dark oak wood, sprawling windows, and crème de la crème chefs. Maybe, that's why I noticed him and felt such empathy; he, too, seemed out of place.

He was an older gentleman overdressed in an inexpensive suit, a three piece, which made him stand out at Sunday morning brunch while most patrons favored dress slacks, or jeans, and a sweater. Seated at my table, he promptly placed the common order of a mimosa. After two whiskey sours, he ordered his food and showed me a picture of his grandkids. There was something vulnerable about him, and I tried to give him a few extra minutes of my time. He ate his breakfast slowly and meticulously requesting more drinks in between bites. At the end of the meal, I placed his bill on the table. We exchanged some more small talk, and I left to finish with other customers.

When I returned to his table, there was no payment. His bill wasn't high, only forty dollars, which he explained to me in a strained voice, he could not pay. As the guilt washed his soft, wrinkled skin in a hue of red, I also recognized in him my old enemy--shame.

I wanted to help him by covering the bill, but I had no tip money yet. Saddened by the thought of exposing him, but too frightened not to report the situation, I reluctantly left his table to inform the manager and hoped she would find a kind way to resolve the dilemma.

As we returned to where he was seated, I was shocked to see him slumped against the wall, thoroughly drunk; only moments before he had carried on a conversation as if completely sober. His suit, I now realized to my astonishment, was out of date, the colors fading, and the areas around the cuffs and buttons fraying.

Like sharks smelling blood, the two restaurant owners were immediately behind us. Helpless, I watched them drag him through the aisles to the front door and throw him into the street. The waitresses were shaking their heads at his audacity and many of the customers were laughing. It was like a scene from a bizarre circus.

"How could you be so stupid!" the older, portly owner demanded of me through his foggy glasses.

"Couldn't you tell he was nothing but a bum?" the tall Irishman, whom I had always admired, bulked incredulously. My heart felt sick with confusion and disappointment as disillusionment set in. 'Who is the bum here?' I thought but couldn't speak. Everyone was staring at me like the main character in a bad play who had forgotten her lines.

When they had gone, the manager walked over to me and, looking at me sensitively, told me not to be afraid of losing my job. She said she would talk to the owners on my behalf. The thought hadn't even occurred to me. In that moment, I didn't care either. Meeting her gaze, I responded bluntly:

"What's going to happen to him? Is he really a bum? Doesn't he have any place to live? He said he had grandchildren!" I started to cry. Her eyes penetrated me for a long moment and then she replied, her words unfolding through a thick accent that added to the otherworldly transcendence of the moment.

"Nicole, you are not like everyone else here. You have a deep compassion. Don't ever change that about yourself." Her kind words strengthened my heart as I tried to absorb my sadness and shock and finish my work.

When my shift was finally over, I stepped out into the chilly darkness of autumn pulling my sweater around me in an attempt to find some comfort from this incredibly exposed and vulnerable feeling I had not been able to shake. I looked for the man, hoping he might still be close by, although I knew he wouldn't be. What had happened that caused him to turn to alcohol? Did he have a friend to whom he could unburden his heart, someone who could see through the crusty surface to uncover the hidden treasure of the man within? Did he need love? Forgiveness? Freedom? Hope? If only I could find him and hear his story, to be like a blanket or a balm to soothe and cover his pain.

I walked home more deliberately than usual, etching into my memory the faces of all the people I passed. Watching them curiously, I experienced a growing tenderness and understanding that every person lives at least two lives; the ones we show on the surface played out on the common streets we all share, and the ones lived out on our interior landscapes, often marked by suffering, disappointment, loneliness and a host of haunting experiences. Perhaps in our own way, we are all lost, our souls struggling with some degree of homelessness.

In that moment, something in my heart broke open, and I could almost see love pouring from me, spreading into the streets, touching people. I longed for them to open up and tell me their stories that I might know them and empathize with them. Somehow the idea made me feel more human, more divine - more whole -, rather than the wandering gypsy I had felt like for so long. On the outside I appeared a normal, young, energetic girl pursuing acting and writing in NYC. But inside, I was broken. I wasn't physically homeless, but I lived constantly on the edge.

I found it difficult, at times impossible, to stay in a romantic relationship with one person for any length of time and although I had many acquaintances, I had no close friends. I used relationships like the grandfather used alcohol- to find acceptance, to forget, to feel loved. We weren't much different, he and I, we were both wounded in some deep way few could see, and yet society treated us so differently because I managed to hide my weaknesses to some extent, while he was detested for his exposing his.

Reaching my building, I took my keys from my pocket. Quickly, I opened the main door and stepped inside as it slammed shut behind me. My steps echoed on the concrete stairs as I made my way to my apartment door. Placing a second key in the lock, I heard the resonation of mechanisms falling into place, stepped into the warm hallway, and closed that door behind me, too. I grabbed a blanket from the chair by my bedroom window and climbed out onto the fire escape. Wrapping the cozy fleece around my shoulders, I found a comfortable seat on a step and peered out into the black sky.

Tomorrow, the playground across the street would be alive with children winding their way through the labyrinth of childhood. Remembering so many classroom exercises of "What do you want to be when you grow up?" I wondered if anyone really makes it to the adulthood they dream of in their youth. Of those who do, what has been the cost? And how many of us are just pretending- going through the motions?

What is the difference between the wife and girlfriend who falsely says "I love you" to keep her home, her money and her comforts and the prostitute in the street who sells a part of herself everyday just to stay alive? Is there a difference between the man in the restaurant today from the alcoholic who hides his addiction behind his job, his nice house, or the cover of his marriage? Maybe, some of us are simply better at hiding than others. Maybe, some of us have someone who loves us despite our flaws, someone who will catch us when we fall, while others are simply alone, and in having to fend for themselves, just can't seem to find their way. Love is what seems to make all the difference.

I looked up at the stars, those small, twinkling celestial bodies resounding in one chord; a mirror of the magnificence humans were meant to be, a light in the darkness, each playing our assigned note, together striking a chord, and ultimately performing as a symphony.

I listened to the sounds of humanity echoing off the tall buildings. Within each window was a person who had a life, a past, memories, thoughts, hopes and dreams. Looking first to the streets below and the few people who still lingered under the old-fashioned lamps, to the houses and all the windows with their small lights on, to the moonlit autumn sky, to the wisps of clouds still visible in the haze of the city luminosity, I knew I was casting more shadow than light, creating more discord than harmony, and decided that whatever it took, I would become whole. And, maybe, the change that was beginning in me tonight would somehow, through God's grace, find its way to the heart of the Grandfather, and help heal him, too.

Lily

It was late afternoon when I reached the small motel on the outskirts of NYC's west side. The sun shone intensely above the stony granite of the dilapidated building, casting a chilling shadow as the winter's night air began its descent. I do not remember how I arrived there, whether by walking, bus or taxi, an absence of memory probably due to the string of traumatic events which forced me to come there in the first place.

Leftover Christmas decorations hung gracelessly in a few windows and doorways. Trash blew aimlessly in the wind, but despite the hour of the day, the neighborhood was otherwise devoid of movement and life. The seedy establishment stood on the corner of an often forgotten, but sadly all too common reality of gloom and hopelessness. A repository for lost souls, of which I was undeniably one, though I wished in my heart I could have said otherwise.

The night before I had stayed in a beautiful resort with my Mom, Aunt, and Nana. They had come to visit me in the city and enjoy a few nights away together. I had shown them all around the vast metropolis, enjoying fancy coffees and beautiful desserts while sitting at window-front tables and watching passersby. I was the youngest of all the kids and grandkids, and it was exciting for them to enjoy family at this new stage of life.

I had not told them that, as of three days prior, I was officially homeless. I was embarrassed and worried what it would do to my Mom to know I had no place to live and how it had all happened. After saying goodbye to them at the train station that afternoon, I had made my way here. Standing outside the dirty building, my face burning with the shame of self-consciousness, I experienced an irrational fear they would suddenly round the corner and see me with my overnight bag hung over my shoulder like a broken limb, disjointed and useless, holding some clothes and one hundred dollars- all I had to my name.

Opening the front door, I was immediately stung by an unfamiliar and eerie presence which held the atmosphere hostage. Though the clock on the wall displayed the accurate hour, it ticked away with a frightening rhythm, as if keeping time for some unseen reality that hung close and threatening. As a naïve woman in her early twenties from a rural middle-class background, I was totally unprepared for the fear that struck me. The thought that I would enter and never leave seemed plausible, but I had nowhere else to go.

The clerk was a man of medium build and dark skin, dressed in a freshly ironed, ruby- colored shirt and tan dress slacks. He glanced up at me over his paper but offered no friendly greeting as did the managers of nicer city hotels. With a growing panic, I shuffled up to the counter. He smiled politely but seemed oddly satisfied when I asked him how much a room would be for the night.

"Twenty-five dollars" he said smugly.

"Okay. I'll pay for two nights" I said handing him fifty dollars in cash.

"Come this way" he said in a low, coy manner as he grabbed a key from a hook behind the desk and lifted the partition. He did not offer to carry my bag and we walked toward the stairs.

A strange smell lingered in the hallway leading to the rooms and the floor was comprised of stained and chipped tiles of once beautiful colors, reds, blues, yellows, and greens. We walked up a flight of stairs, around a corner and down another hallway where he pointed to a dimly lit room that was the bathroom. After passing several more doors, he opened a small, thin door on the right. I will remember that door as long as I live. Dirty and flimsy, strange, and foreign, a doorway to the awful fate that could have been mine permanently if grace had not entered first.

"This is your room."

He stood to the side waiting for me to enter, his countenance a thinly veiled look of lust mingled with curiosity. I almost didn't, it was such a scary place. Standing there, willing myself to go in, I saw out of the corner of my eye, a door left slightly ajar at the end of the hallway. A man and woman sat on a bed, leering at me. Shivers went down my spine. I diverted my eyes from their fixed gaze and went quickly into my room and shut the door. There was little comfort there.

A box spring and mattress with two pillows in white, threadbare, stained cases stood against the wall, covered with a plain sheet, its pallor spread out like a blanket over a corpse. An uneven mirror hung above an old dresser which warped my reflection into an object on a wavy sea. One window was set deep in the corner.

Alone in the room, I dropped my bag by the dresser and thought, half-heartedly, about putting my clothes away, but decided against it. Being here was not a good idea and I was determined not to stay long. Outside the window, the city lights were turning on. I looked back and forth over the night sky for any sign of familiarity, but there was nothing recognizable on the horizon tonight, only warehouses and the lonely lights of the sparse inhabitants of a commercial district.

Beyond my door, music and voices were building in a steady crescendo, as the residents of the hotel were slowly waking up for the night. I thought of the man and woman down the hall and wondered what they would be doing. Unwanted thoughts came to mind. Getting up from the window, I walked over to the door to make sure it was locked securely. It was made of paper-thin material and I knew, with frightening clarity, there was not much standing between me and the comings and goings in the rest of the building. My stomach churned as I secured the little hook-and-eye latch that was all I had to lock the door. I never felt so far from home before. Exhausted with fear and grief, I sat on the bed, and leaned against the wall. Perhaps in the morning life would look better, hope would rise again, and an answer would break forth. Just as I was allowing these thoughts to comfort me, my eyes caught words, written in pencil in the corner of the opposite wall. I leaned forward to read them.

"Just because you're paranoid doesn't mean someone isn't following you."

'How true' I thought with a shiver. I'd been running in fear most of my life, always looking over my shoulder for the next person who would betray my trust and hurt me. Unable to separate those who genuinely loved me from the abuse of my past, I had run from good people, too. I felt sad for the person who wrote this. I was still afraid of the other people in the motel. The energy was thick with depravity here. I could smell it in the air. But I could relate. Wounds bleed, and blood attracts predators. Saying a silent prayer, wrapped tightly in my coat, I finally drifted off to asleep.

All night long, shouts from the corridor and repeated poundings on my paper-thin door interrupted my sleep. Afraid of the dark, I left the light on. Its brightness stabbed me in the eyes every time the noise woke me until, finally, I gave up trying to rest. I spent the remainder of the night poised by the door, ready to punch anyone who tried to break through.

Around four in the morning, the noise started to quiet down. Doors were closing, music was made low, and the motel took on a semi-peaceful quiet. I stood still, taking in small breaths, listening for any sound or movement.

About an hour later, the morning sun spilled gently through the window, like an egg yolk slipping through the cracks of its white shell, it poured into the room, warm and welcoming. I breathed a small sigh of relief.

My bag lay slumped by the dresser where I left it the night before. I dug into it grabbing my toothbrush and hairbrush and put them into my coat pocket. I looked out through the crack in the door for any signs of life. Just as I was going to open the door to run out, I was gripped by one of the most beautiful, sweet voices I ever heard. She spoke into the quiet of the morning in such a way that I saw, in my mind's eye, a soft light like a glowing candle. The voice was like that of a mother to a child, and filled me, for a moment, with the sense that, in spite of how things appeared, all was well.

"Christine." The voice sang out in a melodious whisper. "Christine, it's time to wake up. We have to go."

Quiet and slow, I leaned my ear against the door, for once glad it was so thin. There was a resigned sadness to the voice so that the words came out breathy, carried on a sigh. But there was also hope with a distinctly nurturing tone. Maybe, it was because the voice was the first kind one I'd heard, and I was adding my own needs to it, but it seemed to me to have a strength like the kind afforded to a person who takes care of others in dark places.

"Come on, Christine. The police are here for us and we have to go." The voice rang out again, hauntingly beautiful. I wandered if I was the only one awake to hear her. Would others hear and be comforted, inspired by this gentle woman? I didn't know who Christine was or why the police were here though I could guess why. For a moment I wanted to open the door and see them. But I remained still and paralyzed with fear in my little room.

If only I had opened the door, stepped into the hallway, and introduced myself, maybe I could have helped. Maybe I could have done or said something to encourage the woman speaking as she was trying to encourage Christine. But I did nothing. And so soon enough I heard the woman called Christine emerge from the room next to mine, the door gently shut, her quiet sobs and the sound of their shoes echoing down the hallway tiles, and then growing more faint as they descended the steps. Regret for having not spoken washed over me. Nevertheless, the courage I heard in her voice emboldened me.

I waited a few more minutes, then wrapping my coat tightly around me, I sprinted into the hallway and out the front door. Running toward the William Esper Acting Studio where I had class three times per week, I called my ex, the one who cheated on me numerous times. The one I swore I would never lower myself to go back to again.

"Jason, does your offer to stay with you for a while still stand?"

"Nicole? Are you okay?"

"Not really. Can you pick me up around 7:00 from this address?"

"Of course, I'm glad you called" he said followed by an expectant pause.

Shutting my eyes against the tears, I responded with the words I knew he wanted to hear, the words I knew I needed to say to secure a home, the words I didn't feel.

"Maybe, this is meant to be. Maybe, this will give us another chance to work things out."

"I'd like that." he said, his voice soft and emotional.

"Me, too" I lied. "Hey, I've got to go. I'll see you at 7:00."

When I returned to the motel later that night, the familiar eeriness and hopelessness was more oppressive than before. Fortunately, I never unpacked my bag. Hurriedly, I gave the room a last glance and ran downstairs. Coming up the stairs was the woman I saw when I first got there the night before. A wave of fear struck me. Would she try to talk to me or make me stay? We passed each other so closely I could smell the slight aroma of her perfume, and see her faint make up over the small purple scars in her complexion well hidden in the rich darkness of her skin.

"Hello." She smiled warmly.

"Hello" I said, my voice faltering as we passed in opposite directions.

My stomach fluttered. It was the woman from this morning. The woman calling for Christine. Stunned, I half stumbled the rest of the way down to where Jason was parked at the curb.

"Here, let me get that for you." He took my bag and loaded it in the back of the car.

My heart was torn. I was so scared and couldn't wait to leave, yet I did not want to go. I wanted to wait for her. Would she talk with me? What would I even say? Why was I so drawn to her? Jason opened the door for me, and I sat inside, but did not close it. The streetlamp glared over the sidewalk where an older style limousine was waiting.

Just then, the woman strode out of the building, her jaw set, chin jutting out, spiked boot heels clicking on the cement. Her demeanor was like stone, but her revealing clothing belied her frail condition.

"Come on, baby! Let's party!" hollered the men from within the dark, cave-like rear area. Their faces hidden, several arms grasped carelessly, greedily, at her small frame and pulled her inside. The door closed with a thud, and they drove away. There were so many of them, and just one of her.

"Nicole, we should go" Jason said knowingly. He had lived here all his life. I was too stunned to move.

I nodded my head but sat motionless, the night engulfed by a strange silence. My lips trembled, but I could not speak. My heart pounded my body shook. Jason put his hand on my shoulder, an invitation to connect I wanted to refuse but couldn't.

"There were so many of them....and just her" I blurted.

"I know."

Willing myself out of the car, I stepped onto the empty sidewalk. A deep sadness swept over me. What was going to happen to her? If only I had opened my door this morning. But what could have I done really? What did I have to offer? I had no money and no place of my own. Still, I should have said something. Standing under the streetlamp, a strange and powerful sense of being lost and found came over me. For the first time in a long time I heard what I believe was God's voice, a whisper into my heart: *I am enthralled with her beauty.*

When God speaks one word, a single sentence, can have a multi-layer meaning. I immediately understood her beauty was also mine, covered over by hard circumstances and inner wounds, but shiningly clear to the Creator of the whole universe. Where we happen to be in life, what grim difficulties we may be experiencing, does not change who we are, the majesty of who we were created to be. God sees us and calls to us. Even when we can't hear or choose not to listen, or other voices drown Him out, He continues His pursuit. Peering in the direction of the limo one last time, I was overcome with both grief and hope. I got the feeling God yearned to reach out and hold her. Wrapping my arms around myself, I got into the car and shut the door against the growing chill.

"Did you know her?" Jason asked gently.

"Yes...no. Not really...She looked out for people here. I didn't even know her name." Later, when I began writing this story, I envisioned her with a Stargazer Lily in her hair, a symbol of her gentleness and beauty even in this awful place. I decided I would call her Lily.

As we drove along toward Jason's apartment, I watched the people in passing cars, the couples strolling hand in hand going to dinner or the theater, others on their way home after a long day's work. Were any of these options within reach to the Lily? Who could she fall back on? Why did some people have safe, wholesome, secure lives while others live in abuse and darkness? My head was full of questions.

Though it would be many years before I fully understood the impact of my one night in that small motel, driving away with Jason I knew I had spent the night uncomfortably close to a prostitute only to realize that prostitute was also me. It had been me for some time. I had moved here determined to become an actress. I had imagined portraying the lives of others, inspiring audiences through theatre and film, would be a noble calling. But the city could be hard, and the profession ruthless. And I had come here already broken. The compromises made because of pain and shame, wanting to be loved, and the fear of being alone, were making a faithless woman out of me.

The truth was Lily and I, like many in this world, were selling ourselves for survival. Whether we are standing on a street corner or going home with someone we know, or whether we are lying to get a promotion, or lying to ourselves and those we love, creating a false life because we are too afraid to pursue the one we dream of, doesn't matter. Yet, we will often judge someone like Lily whose life is exposed, while overlooking our own sin and shame that we try to hide.

God was showing me what was in my heart and He wanted me to know I did not need to be anyone extraordinary to be whole, successful, or loved. I just needed to be me. I already was loved. He was enthralled with his daughters' beauty.

I also knew I had to be honest with Jason. I had to tell him I didn't love him anymore. Though I had loved him deeply at one time, ongoing infidelity had destroyed any feeling I had left, and it wasn't right to pretend otherwise. If he let me stay with him until I got on my feet that would be great. If not, I would figure something else out or I would move home. Either way, we both deserved the truth.

A friend drove me back to the motel several times over the next few months, but I never found Lily. I do not know what happened to her. I shudder to think if she ever made it back safely that night. As for me, it would be several more years until I would finally become the woman I began dreaming I could be that night. And I am still becoming her. I have also been blessed with a loving husband, children, and a good life.

For the last twenty years, I have been supporting organizations that free women from the sex trade. Every time another beautiful woman is rescued, given a safe place to live, helped with school or a job, and told she is loved, I think of Lily.

And hear her sweet voice speaking into the dawn of a new morning, illuminating the darkness with light.

Hero or Criminal

*I*n my mid-twenties I was a barmaid for a local seaside tavern on the Gold Coast of Long Island. By day, the place had a certain worn wayfarer's charm. But by night, when wives came looking for stray husbands and tired children were propped up in corners, when money for the family was instead in the till, I often hated my job and myself.

Frankie, an older man in his fifties and one of my regulars, kept me grounded. He saw the good in me and believed one day I would leave the pub and do something meaningful with my life. At that time, I was deeply interested in the culture of Native American people and was sharing some of what I was learning with Frankie who listened with his usual discerning attentiveness.

"Why do you like them so much?" he said cajoling me with his heavy Italian accent. "That's all you talk about anymore." Taking a deep drag from his cigarette, he waited for me to reply as the smoke curled around his face adding to the otherworldly feel of the night atmosphere.

"Many reasons, but mostly because I want to live my life with the same freedom and integrity they did." I leaned over the whirling glass washer my eyes smarting with tears.

"You know" he said as he rolled his cigarette between his fingertips, "that's what Anthony says. Chief Sitting Bull is his favorite and," he took a long pause, "he wants out of the family business." He stared at me intently, watching how I would react to this new information.

"I was wondering if we were ever going to talk about who you worked for. It's not like I didn't know your employer is the biggest mafia boss in New York."

"I know that you know!" Frankie waved his cigarette in the air, his macho side seeking to regain control of the conversation now that his cover was blown.

"Mama Mia comma downa" I said making fun of him as I usually did in such moments.

Frankie's official role was that of handy man. However, he was more a confidante who had emigrated from Italy to be with the family in whatever benign capacity they might need. To my knowledge, he was never involved in any criminal activities, but I didn't ask, and he didn't tell. I was his friend away from that life and we both understood the boundaries.

"So, you are not bothered about who I work for?"

"Look, I don't know a lot about the mafia or your boss, but I do know that some of these guys who work as pharmaceutical reps, living in mansions with heated driveways while poor people around the world die because they don't have proper medical care, are also types of criminals in my book."

"What you say is true" Frankie said as he extinguished his cigarette. "And, so, do you believe Anthony is telling the truth?"

"He's your boss. What do you think?" My response was intentionally flippant.

"I know what I think, little lady. Don't play games with me! I'm asking you because I trust your judgment. And you should feel lucky." He had this way of glaring and smiling at me simultaneously. We were a good match for each other.

"Many people feel like prisoners in their own lives, Frankie. Most have the desire to live free. I don't know Anthony personally, but I think the way the Native Americans lived - and died - for freedom, for their families, for their land and way of life, inspires people."

Frankie lit another cigarette, going into deep-thought mode as I mixed a few drinks for new customers. On my next shift, I brought in one of my favorite books on Native Americans for Frankie to give to Anthony.

"I think he already has this one, but I'll give it to him."

"Thank you. I put a little note in there." And no more was said.

Several weeks later, Frankie was walking me home when Anthony and several other men drove up the street. We stopped on the curb where the sporty SUV slowed and came to a halt. Even in the dark of night a considerable shadow lingered over the men and their vehicle.

"Hello" he said with a mellow voice that lilted through the fall air. "It's a little late to be walking this young lady around the streets, Frankie." The men in the car laughed.

I was surprised at how serene Anthony's voice was. Naively, I suppose, I had expected a gangster to speak in a tone of gravel and grave. Thoughts of how different this meeting could be if I was someone on the wrong side of them crossed my mind.

"Thank you for the book" he said.

"Frankie thought you already had that one. Sorry about that." I stood awkwardly as the men in the car eyed me, probably suspicious of my intentions. They appeared as an oppressive chain around him. I didn't know where they were off to, but I was grateful to be heading home to my books and tea.

In the diffused glow of the streetlamp, Anthony's eyes brimmed with gentleness and longing. It felt strange really ~ the boss of the biggest organized crime family in New York and a barmaid from a little pub in a small New York town, both searching for the courage to live the life we envisioned and wondering if it was even possible. The whole thing seemed surreal, but so *real* all the same. Anthony made a joke to shift the mood.

"Frankie, you told her I had the book? I can't trust you with anything." Frankie blushed. He was getting a playful scolding tonight. "You get her home safe, Frankie. Good man."

The two men exchanged looks. Frankie had been a gentleman to me since we met, always walking me to my doorstep when I worked the night shift. We moved on as the men drove away. I marveled silently to myself at God's providence. How many times had He surrounded me with protection? He was even using the mafia to look after me.

I saw Anthony several times after that, and although few words were spoken between us, I always felt compelled to say a prayer for him and his family, and myself that our hidden longings would come true. God has a unique way of answering prayers, sometimes, though. Within the next year, I had given birth to a baby girl, and Anthony was in jail. Though both situations were difficult, and I'm guessing not the way either of us would have chosen or imagined, these roads ultimately led to our freedom.

Shortly after my daughter was born, I began going to church, and when she was only a few years old, I was invited to attend a church up the road from where I lived. At that time, I was still teetering between the Jesus taught to me by my Grandmother as a child, and the open road of the different religions I had followed in my late teens and early twenties. I almost didn't go, but the neighbor who had invited me was a little girl, and I felt I couldn't let her down. That Sunday was a turning point in my life.

After the service, they were having a spaghetti dinner. The Pastor announced if there were any guests visiting that they were welcome to stay and have lunch – for free. As a single Mom, on a tight budget, the idea of a free lunch for me and my daughter was a welcome invitation. But there was something else.

Before the Pastor offered lunch to us, he had paused. It was the pause that had gotten my attention. It was not a pause of reluctance, but of listening, as if he hadn't planned on extending the invitation, but had been told to do so just in that instant. In his moment of waiting, which lasted only a few seconds, I felt an electrifying feeling of anticipation, and then the most intense feeling of love, of being home, washed over me. Immediately, I wanted to go to that spaghetti dinner. In fact, I felt it would be the most amazing thing I had done in a long time. I almost laughed out loud at the idea of that. And, yet, I was filled with wonder, too.

For almost two years, I attended church there, being loved on by the women, and falling more in love with Jesus every day. It was the end of the old life, and the beginning of the new. I was baptized and filled with the Holy Spirit. Although the road has been so challenging, it has been the road of freedom and integrity I longed for.

A few years ago, I did some research and discovered Anthony did leave the mafia. It took many years, the darkness does not let go easily, but he is now living his life as the husband and father he wanted to be. Others might still judge him a criminal, but when I saw the radiant faces of his wife and children, I am sure they believed he was a hero.

So often, we feel caught in our lives and believe there is no way out. Many, with less barriers than Anthony, stay trapped in circumstances they could change with enough time and faith. Jesus is faithful, and He will do it. There is no situation too hard for Him.

The Perfect Gift

I had recently moved back to my hometown of York, Pennsylvania after living away for over a decade. It was good to be around family and familiar faces and to make a fresh start after a time of difficulty. I enrolled in school and worked part-time at the mall in one of the largest stores which sold everything from clothing to cookware, toys and sweets. The Christmas season arrived adding to my enthusiasm.

The mall was decorated to the hilt. Lights sparkled and lawn-size blow up snow men with fake snowfall crowded the doorways. Colorful cards brimmed over in isles, tall Christmas trees shimmered with bulbs and tinsel, and shop windows were dressed in seasonal flare. In our store was a special section just for ornaments, old fashioned villages, and other nostalgic Christmas pieces. Everything was set for a perfect Christmas.

One bitter, cold evening while working the register, a beautiful young woman came behind the counter to help.

Striking black raven hair, deep green eyes and a mischievous grin, she couldn't have been older than sixteen, but her presence was powerful. I almost didn't notice she was missing part of her left arm, from the mid forearm down.

Trying not to stare, I smiled more awkwardly than I hoped impulsively taking another glance at her arm. Sticking out her chin, she stared me down as if to say if I was going to work with her, I'd better not be entertaining thoughts of pity.

To accent her unspoken point, she grabbed a shopping bag and sliced it through the air. Holding it open with her stump, she began putting the purchased items in the bag, flashing an impish grin to the customer, who being a regular, returned the smile over her brown rimmed glasses while paying her bill. When the customer left, we formally introduced ourselves.

"I'm Julie. I hear that you're new" she said.

"Hi. I'm Nicole. I started a few weeks ago. I take it you've worked here a while."

"Yeah, but only on holidays during the school year."

"What grade are you in?" I asked.

"Junior" she said and smiled, cocking her petite face to one side. "How about you?" We laughed.

"I just moved home from New York. I have a four-year-old daughter."

We locked eyes for a long moment and then spent the rest of the night getting to know each other in between helping shoppers.

Julie was a hard worker. She had trouble with certain tasks but wouldn't be helped. She showed amazing ingenuity in solving problems that arose due to her disability. She was open and friendly, and fun to work with, but always there seemed to linger a red rim of sadness around her eyes as if she cried recently or was on the verge of doing so.

"I live with my Dad and little brother" she revealed one quiet night when the ice and snow had kept most customers away. She spoke of her Dad as a gentle soul with a big heart, a stable and loving man.

"Where's your Mom?" I asked gently, unsure of the reaction my question might elicit, and not wanting to hurt my new friend.

"She left us when we were little." Her voice broke with the weight of unanswered questions.

Caught off guard, I didn't know what to say. I waited to see if Julie would elaborate on possible reasons for her Mom's exit from the family, but she didn't offer any, and I didn't ask.

"What are you doing for Christmas?" she said changing the subject.

"We go to church on Christmas morning and then to my Grandma's for dinner. What about you?"

"Same." She said with a faraway look in her eye.

"Have you ever gone into York City to hear the steam whistles at the York Wire Co. on Christmas Eve?" I asked, feeling a possible adventure coming on.

"No, what's that?" Julie smiled, perking up.

"The owner of the company uses the factory whistles to play Christmas carols. It's not something I can explain. You have to hear them for yourself. I've never experienced anything like them anywhere."

"I would love to go."

We agreed to meet at the mall, and I would drive us to the city.

Christmas Eve arrived clear and frigid. Heading into York we sang carols and admired the lights and festive decorations. By the time we arrived at the York Wire Co. we were well into the spirit of the season. Sitting quietly in the warmth of the car, sipping steaming hot cappuccinos, an awkward silence fell over us for the first time in our friendship. The holiday cheer seemed to amplify what we both felt we were lacking in life.

I was almost eighteen years older than Julie. Technically, she could have been my daughter. A part of me wanted to ask if I could fill that motherly role for her in some small way, or a big sister would be an honor, too. I loved her so much. But the reality was that I'm a wayfarer by nature and didn't know how long I'd be in York. My own life, torn at the seams, was only slowly mending. And something in my heart, though I couldn't say exactly what, was not completely convinced that was my purpose for meeting Julie.

What I knew was that her strength in adversity, her lack of self-pity, and her spunky spirit had brought a bright light into my life. I had never had a physical disability, but I'd often felt disabled internally, in my mind and emotions, as a result of childhood pain. Neither her limb deformity, nor my mental health struggles, would just "go away." Being with Julie gave me courage to honor that.

Likewise, my special interest in her, to tell her with certainty of her value as a woman, and that a woman's wholeness, came from far more than her physical self, brought her the gift of a certain peace. The validation that she was truly one of the most beautiful girls I had ever seen, physically and spiritually, gave her a fresh perspective, a new self-love in her circumstances.

For the last month we had witnessed the frenzy of gift buying. Some people had experienced joy finding just the right gift for a loved one, a child or friend. But many had worn haggard and hassled looks, made comments that belied their resentment in spending money on people they didn't really care for and money they didn't really have.

Julie and I hadn't bought each other any ugly scarves, cheap perfume, or CDs that neither fit our personality or interests. We hadn't bought each other anything at all. We had given of ourselves - our love and friendship, a safe place to be who we were, and be accepted. We had given each other the gift of presence bearing witness to the other's life. Our friendship was one of my favorite gifts of the season. It occurred to me that was what Jesus gave people, too. And what He still gives- the holy gift of His presence. Our friendship was really His gift, and He was there with us to unwrap and enjoy it.

Just as I was about to ask Julie what she was thinking, the steam whistles opened to play their first carol of the night sky. We stepped out of the car, and into a song, the name forgotten now, but the sound remembered forever. Notes like a slide whistle, sung slightly exaggerated and off key, beautiful and otherworldly. Julie stood in awe as the whistles resounded off the buildings.

Taking the risk, I reached out and wrapped my arm around her little limb. She looked up at me with her classic smile. As the whistles played on, I understood, Christmas, or any season of life, isn't about finding perfect - a gift, family or life. Perhaps perfect comes from giving the imperfect gift of ourselves, those parts of all of us that are off-key ~ our true song. The one playing in the dissonance between what we believe life should be and what it is.

As if in affirmation, a puff of steam poured over the buildings, above the streetlights. And for a moment I saw in my mind's eye the factory organist at his instrument of whistles, sharing his gift, smiling at the joy of his unique labor. Silent Night echoing now, breathing into the dreams of the city.

Eye of the Beholder

I met Lilah in my second year of college in an English class. In a windowless room, packed to the brim on a cool autumn morning, the teacher had challenged us to share our fears. After a few confessions of the typical type- spiders, failing, etc. she raised her hand and offered her story.

"I hate having surgeries" she said her voice a mixture of defiance and grief. "I've had so many of them to correct my eyes and face. It's to the point that as soon as I'm in the elevator on the ride up I can smell the operating room and anaesthesia and I start remembering what it feels like to go under. I'm tired of going under. And I'm afraid." Her lyrical voice softened to pianissimo.

Lilah was born with Sturge-Weber Syndrome, a rare congenital neurological and skin disorder which affected her sight and covered most of her face with a large purple birthmark. I had seen her around campus and, for reasons unknown to me at the time, had been inexplicably drawn to her.

"What are you afraid of most, Lilah?" the teacher asked with the gentle probing of a consummate professional, yet the genuine concern of a close friend. He was tall and handsome, with warm, soft features and a winsome way about him that made discussing the jagged terrain of fear intriguing, even appealing. Lilah took a brave emotional step toward the cliff.

"I'm afraid the surgeries will never stop." She halted, tears welling, lips quivering.

"And what will happen if the surgeries never stop?" he asked, compassionately pursuing her for the deeper truths. As if pierced in the heart words tumbled out, gushing rivulets of truth, cleansing, healing, devastating.

"I'm afraid I'll never find love!" The room rang with her heart's cry. Tears flowed. "I want to know love. I want to be romanced by the man of my dreams. The surgeries are to help me heal, make me beautiful. But they never stop. There's no happy ever after with them - just another surgery and another and another."

They say tears are messengers to heaven. I believe heaven's door must have flung wide open that day. Almost everyone in the room was crying. My own face felt aflame as I listened to Lilah's cries take flight with longing and passion; hot tears poured in streams down my cheeks, unstoppable from the deep places within.

I was not just listening to a classmate, but to a kindred spirit. Someone who spoke my heart language. Someone whose identity had also been damaged in her search for beauty and love. I did not wear the mark of my wounds on my face. Mine were branded on my heart and soul. Hearing her speak in such courageous, vivid truth shocked me wide open. I imagined many in the room could have told their own version of the story.

I had been sexually abused as a child which had marred me with shame and self-loathing. In my teens and early twenties, the elixir of outward attractiveness and inner brokenness elicited all the wrong attention.

I didn't go to college after high school like most of my friends. I hadn't had the courage or belief in myself. Instead, I had moved to New York City to study acting and writing, to flee from my tumultuous and shameful past and get lost in the anonymity of millions of people. I didn't understand the way shame and wounding follow you and soon my life fell into the old patterns.

The surgeries in my search for love included relationships, alcohol, drugs, counselling, more counselling, medicine, religion, and too many other wayward trails not worth mentioning, but just like Lilah I always went under, too.

After having my daughter in my late twenties, I moved home believing my life was over. Instead, I discovered becoming a mother had given me the confidence to go to college and believe I could be successful. If I could manage a household, then surely I could pass a few classes.

I had also forsaken religion for a true, life-giving relationship with Christ. Something about the way He loved me, His people loved each other, made me believe. Something in the way the Apostle Paul said we are like jars of clay with this indescribable treasure within us. I could see it, like stars in the black night sky. The revelation had made me brave, made me want to stop hiding.

Everything had been going great. I was at the top of my class and got along well with my professors. Then, at my yearly medical check-up, I had been diagnosed with precancerous cells in my cervix and was scheduled for surgery. Another violation, another raw reminder of the consequences of being abused and the self-destructive choices that followed.

I had been single for almost seven years, waiting for the man God had in mind for me as a husband, if it were to be. Now, the longings of my heart for marriage and family felt more elusive than ever. My identity seemed forever entangled in the ugliness of my past. I felt like I was falling into a mountainous cavern with no way to break the fall- and then Lilah shared her story - and suddenly there was hope.

A few weeks later, she and I were in another class together. I asked her if we could meet for coffee. We arranged a time and spent the hour in endless conversation. I felt a thrill in her presence, strength in her spirit. I learned she was a sister in Christ, we shared the same Father. Maybe, He had brought us together for a reason. Maybe, it was the fact that Lilah couldn't hide her wound that lent me the courage to reveal mine. Like Jesus stretched out across that cross naked, nothing to cover His wounds, yet He despised the shame for the joy set before Him. Our identity, marred on earth in our own eyes, still we were joy to Him. His openness, her openness, called to me.

"I have to go for surgery, too, next week" I heard myself blurting. I waited. She nodded encouragingly. A slow, layer by layer purging followed of my history of abuse and relationship failures. She didn't flinch but continued to chew on her salad.

"I've never even been kissed." A wry smile crossed her face, longing too without judgment. She looked at me and nodded again. "It's the same thing, really. Too much and not enough. Both leave you feeling empty."

"Yes. I think so" I whispered.

Right then, with the golden sun of autumn cascading across our table, I wanted to cup her face. I imagined her birthmark would pulse with life right there in my hand, holding me as I held her. Our beauty, still furled, would one day be released, even now was being released, like the leaves dropping from trees.

"Curse this undertow" I laughed through tears.

"It's not taking us down anymore." She stared at me intense like someone who'd received a vision, a revelation of sorts. And that descending light, stepping down from heaven, broke upon us there where grief and hope mingled, and held us, the beautiful beloved, in the eye of the Beholder,

In the waning sunlight I searched the eyes of so many surgeries expecting to see landscapes of war-torn countries. Instead they were eloquent, watery deep dug wells. They would bring refreshment for the prince who drank their first kiss.

As for me, I decided this surgery would be a new beginning, my own new well where the true me would spring up. I could almost see my reflection there, shining.

Just Like You and Me

Though it was still early morning, the black road shimmered as the sweltering Virginia heat snaked upwards like a fizzling firecracker. The sweet scent of lemon verbena, which had been potent through Richmond, faded to an untraceable presence the closer I drove to Fluvanna. Lush southern hospitality turned dry and dusty as the last leg of the journey on Route 250 West ended abruptly in front of the Fluvanna Women's Correctional Center.

The prison was small by most standards, housing only a little over a thousand inmates. Its flat box shape doled out oppression, dead ends, and nothingness. It was hard to believe the souls of over a thousand women were confined there.

Before I made it to the front door, a prison guard stopped me; her black hair pulled into a tight, slick bun bringing her sharp dark eyes into halt-inducing focus.

"Your bra strap is showing. Do you have another shirt?"

she said, not so much a question as a statement as blunt as the intruding heat already causing me to wither.

I looked over at my shoulder where a tiny sliver of elastic poked out from under my dress, a simple knee-length specifically chosen for its classy, non-sexual appearance. I pushed the strap the millimeter back under the material.

"Not good enough," she retorted. "You need a shirt, or you aren't going in."

Slogging back to the car, I drove another five miles before I came to a small-town grocery store with a tiny clothing section. After fifteen minutes of fruitlessly searching for something that would complement the dress, I chose a large, brown men's shirt for five dollars.

Back at the prison, when I was through the metal detector, interviewed and officially checked in, I noticed three older women who were allowed to enter with see-through t-shirts exposing dark bras and some flesh, standing defiantly in front of me, like immature school girls who cheated their way to the front of the line. Their leader smirked at me, a glimmer of greasy sweat above her overly lip - sticked mouth. This must have been their usual Saturday outing and I couldn't help but feel a little pity for them with their grey hair. Who knew how long they'd been at this, visiting daughters, granddaughters, lovers behind prison walls? Still, I didn't appreciate being targeted and inconvenienced while they got a free pass.

We boarded the bus that would take us to the main site. One tall, wired gate after another opened with a buzz as the old, green box of metal lumbered through the obstacle course constructed to keep prisoners from escaping.

Just Like You and Me ▪ 45

The blue sky hung like glass above, as if mirroring all the unobtainable dreams of women now locked inside, like clouds just drifting in circles, dispersing.

"Are you here to visit family?" the bus driver asked, seeming to sense my nervousness.

"No. My pen-pal. We've been writing for several years and today is the first time we're going to meet each other."

I exhaled audibly and felt better. A smile crossed my face as I realized that after all this time, our meeting was only a few short minutes away. The bus driver looked at me for a moment, studying my excitement.

"I wish everyone saw these women like you do. Most of them are just like you and me, ya know. Just had more trouble along the way, maybe. Many with no family. No friends. No one to give them a little direction." She shook her head.

"That's true," I said quietly thinking about some of the personal circumstances Rebecca shared with me in her letters.

Dust blew from the wheels in a puff as the bus stopped with a heavy sigh in front of the entrance. Several security guards escorted us to the waiting area while others collected inmates from their cells. Rebecca and I wrote about this day for so long. Now, it was finally happening. Waiting for our scheduled time, I thought about how God brought Rebecca and I together.

Three years prior, I prayed for direction in my writing life. I took courses, stuffed a filing cabinet and other boxes with poems, short stories, a book manuscript, and several drafts of a screenplay. I published in a few places but felt as though I couldn't gain traction. *Where should I put my focus?* I wondered. Small or big, it didn't matter; just an opportunity to write regularly for someone, somewhere, was all I asked.

The answer arrived out of the blue one stray day on the back page of a Prison Fellowship newsletter I didn't even remember signing up for; a plea for pen-pals for over one thousand men and women on a waiting list, most of whom would never receive a pen-pal because there weren't enough volunteers.

At first, I resisted. "No, Lord" I said out loud even as the need pulled at my heartstrings. "This isn't what I had in mind." I was a single Mom working several jobs and did not have the time or energy for more volunteer work. "I need to make money. I need my needs met instead of this endless expending." But there was no point. I knew in my heart this was the answer to my prayer. I filled out the form and sent it away. Within a few months, I received the information for my pen-pal, Rebecca. We had an immediate kinship, and after three years of letters, we were now going to meet in person.

Rebecca and I had a lot in common. We were close in age and loved to write and read. We were both mothers, although Rebecca hadn't seen her son in years, and the authorities placed her infant daughter in foster care.

"I was pregnant when I got to jail," she wrote. "When the time came for my baby to be born, they hand-cuffed me to the bed. Then took her as soon as it was over. I never even got to hold her. She's been adopted."

I admit that I didn't believe her at first. I figured there must have been something terribly wrong with her parenting for them to just take her baby away like that. But after doing some research I learned it could happen just as Rebecca said, especially the being hand-cuffed part, although many jails now have mother and baby units where children can stay for various amounts of time. Other letters contained her distress over her son.

"My ex-husband won't bring him to see me. I don't even know if he's okay. He must be so ashamed of me. What if he doesn't love me anymore? Can you write to him if I give you the address?"

I wrote several times, though neither of us ever got a response.

Despite this, and a difficult childhood where she endured a broken family, abuse, and loneliness, she was, surprisingly, lacking in self-pity. Instead, she focused on self-improvement and helping others. She was also deeply compassionate and wise. I enjoyed writing to her about my life and always appreciated the sage advice she gave me.

"God made you just the way you are because that's how He wanted you... He has a plan for your life, and you don't have to worry about how things are going to turn out... We only have this one day. Enjoy it... Stop fighting with your daughter all the time. Hug her."

We also learned we were both victims of childhood sexual abuse. Both perpetrators were family members. Both of us used drugs, alcohol and relationships to numb the pain. She robbed a convenience store for drug money. I didn't because drugs were always provided for me. Or I could have been where she was. Most of the people I knew could have been where she was.

I didn't judge her for being in jail, and she didn't judge me for not being there. I understood how hard it was for her sometimes to hear about my daughter and the things we did together, the freedoms we enjoyed. She also understood that sometimes I envied her, not for being in jail, but for having the quiet time she did, time to think and dream and write, without all the responsibilities of working, cooking, cleaning and raising a child alone. We let each other breathe. We let each other be.

We shared many intimate details through our letters. I was anxious to see if the authenticity of our relationship would transcend pen and paper. Waiting with the other visitors, I imagined Rebecca, in her cell, wondering the same.

A sad-looking older man, a father perhaps, looked at my awkward fitting t-shirt, then at the women in their white shirts, and shook his head. I sensed he wanted to talk, but the presence of the guards was like a mute button. I suppose we were all concerned we would say or do the wrong thing and not be allowed in to see our loved ones.

Time seemed to tick slow and heavy. Even in the airconditioning, the southern heat slinked through the sealed windows, sapping strength, and settling on the chest like a smothering, unwanted blanket. Shifting my weight from one hip to the other and back again, I became aware that my excitement and anticipation, were turning to fear and discomfort. I felt a chill though the room grew increasingly humid and suffocating.

I had come all this way. Why was I suddenly getting cold feet now? I visited inmates before; prison environments didn't intimidate me. Rebecca and I wrote to one another for a long time, we called each other *friend*. So, what was bothering me?

Through a strange heaviness, long forgotten memories began to resurface. Rebellious teenage nights of stealing from cars left unlocked in our sleepy, trusting town. Starker memories of my friends and I slashing car seats and tires of boys who used us then tossed us aside. Sad memories, the ignored pleading messages of a close friend who lost his job and desperately needed payback on the money he'd lent me. For a woman who prided herself on honesty, the image of a younger me hiding in the corner of my apartment while the voice mail rattled and hissed with human pain was almost unbearable. God can choose the most unsuspected times to unearth our sins.

Waiting on the sandy-colored tiles, I found myself under a heavy fire of self-scrutiny. My foot, which was unconsciously tracing the floor's patterns stopped, and pressed flat against the floor, looking for gravity, and grounding. *Who had committed the worst crime?* Rebecca, for stealing to support a drug habit. A habit she began to drive away the demons of severe child abuse inflicted upon her and her brothers by a stepfather. Or me, for robbery without motive, petty revenge, or betraying someone who trusted me?

Comparing wrongs doesn't make anyone right, but who should determine what transgressions deserve this warehousing of human souls, while others barely attract a second thought. It all seems so black and white until you're the one on the free side of the fence facing a thousand lives and their families, and it feels like each one is asking you "How is this fair?"

I could have easily traded places with Rebecca, and it would have been just. All this time, I was encouraging her to forgive herself, to receive God's forgiveness, and move on. Yet here I was the one needing to forgive myself and receive forgiveness for sins hidden deep in my past.

With a sigh of relief, grace coursed through my veins. I turned away from the guards to hide the tears of release streaming down my face. I did not want them to think something was wrong and start asking questions. But how good it felt. I could breathe again.

A loud buzzer sounded as doors clunked open on the opposite side of the visitors' room. A rowdy rumble quickly filled the large gymnasium and spilled into the corridor as the women entered talking and calling to one another. Underneath the laughter were a subtle but tangible anger and sorrow, the wounds of caged songbirds, of stolen dreams.

Their refrains grabbed my heart with unseen, yet palpable, hands. These were sisters, mothers, daughters, aunts, grandmas. Though we were strangers, I knew them, and they knew me. Our roads were different, but the same. We walked the long road of night and I felt in that moment the truth of it in my flesh and blood. This, too, is like God who awakens us to our own truth, who calls us to lay down the masks we wear for self-preservation and blesses us with kinship in the most unlikely of places. Gone was the fear. The joy and anticipation of seeing Rebecca returned.

A stern, baritone female voice came loudly through an overhead speaker ordering everyone to "Be quiet and take your seats!" Suddenly, the volume in the room softened. Squeaking chairs slid against the floor as the women took their seats. The buzzer sounded again and with a loud mechanical boom our door unlocked, and we followed instructions to enter, quickly find our inmate, and sit down. *Poor Rebecca*, I thought. *What a terrible way to live.*

Thrown a bit off balance, but so thrilled to be here finally to meet Rebecca, I quickly scuttled through the door and scanned the room. I almost didn't recognize her, her face was paler than in her pictures, with heavier make-up around her eyes, and a shorter haircut. But when our eyes locked, I knew her immediately. Present was that same spirit to spirit connection we shared through the years of letter writing.

She was sitting at a little table with two chairs, one on either side, a huge smile on her face and eyes filled with hope. I made a beeline for her and immediately wrapped my arms around her in a tight embrace. She hugged me back but felt stiff and kept a distance with the rest of her body. Before I could respond a voice screeched into the microphone.

"No touching!" I immediately let go and turned in the direction of the command. The officer was glaring at us. I took a step back, my face flushed with embarrassment. I wanted to help Rebecca but was already drawing unwanted- and unneeded- attention to my dear friend.

"I'm sorry, Rebecca," I muttered earnestly, taking my seat.

"It's okay," she said, trying not to smile too wide as we were still being watched but with a hint of mischief in her eyes that let me know she shared in the joy of our little "crime." "They think everyone in here is a lesbian and in their minds all lesbians think about is sex, so they don't even let us hug each other." She rolled her eyes.

Rebecca was serving a thirteen-year sentence. Was she really expected to go without physical touch for thirteen years? The repercussions on her mind, body and soul would be devastating. She said many prisoners turn to sexual activity with other inmates and even guards, not only to satisfy natural sexual desires, but also to simply be held. Having been a single mom for seven years, I knew that yearning well.

"Let's get some food," I said, spotting the vending machine. Over a smorgasbord of candies, chips and soda, we spent the next two hours talking serious and silly in a conversation that transcended time. We shared our fears and laid them to rest. We agreed I would contact her son again. We shared our hope that one day we would both meet a man and fall in love and, most of all, that one day our pains and struggles would be used to help others.

"I feel like everything's going to be okay, Nicole." She looked at me with big brown eyes.

"Me, too, Rebecca." Our eyes lingered over one another's face, a soul to soul presence, separated by human law but meeting on common ground.

In Rebecca's presence, I felt redeemed. My heartache and life's mistakes were not the misshapen wanderings of a failed soul, but a path with purpose, no doubt riddled with darkness, confusion and wrong turns, but noble and beautiful, nevertheless. My prayer for writing opportunities didn't lead to a regular paying job, but they begot purpose, true life-giving purpose that feeds the spirit.

We were not doomed, useless or unlovable. Indeed, sitting in the prison visiting room, we were more grace-filled than ever. Looking at Rebecca, listening to her talk, with the other women prisoners all around us, I felt like God spared me from something. Not from prison, or losing my children, or the black mark that comes from being an inmate, although I was humbled and my gratitude for my own life renewed when I saw firsthand how hard Rebecca had it.

I felt like God spared me from a mediocre, narrow-minded life, from the "not knowing" of how others live and suffer. Not only how they suffer, but how we all long, dream, fear and hope. Every woman in that room, full of promise and purpose, is just like you and me. More than that, I felt I was spared from the" not *wanting* to know" because it's too uncomfortable, too close to home, too inconvenient. And I just knew it wasn't something I did for myself. This knowing, this wanting to know, was somehow beyond me, somehow chosen for me, and I felt so grateful.

"Do you want to get our picture taken together?" she asked me, pointing to the photo area with the background to make it look like an outdoor shot.

"Sure!" We walked over like we were flying.

I was a bit taller than Rebecca. So, at the last moment before the shot, I bent down and leaned in, briefly touching her, shoulder to shoulder. She looked up at me and smiled. Then we both smiled into the camera. When our picture was printed, we ran back to our table like two giddy schoolgirls. Our joy was short-lived, however.

"Visiting for today is over! All visitors make your way to the blue doors!"

"It's time for you to go." Her face was drawn and sad.

"I hate leaving you here." Tears smarted in my eyes as I clenched my jaw determined that no pity would cross my face. She didn't need or deserve that.

"You came. That's enough...for now." She laughed through tears, which made me laugh through my own tears.

"I'll write to you as soon as I get home. And I'll be back."

"Okay." There was nothing left to do but to turn and go.

In my next letter I told her I put our picture on my desk. She hung hers in her cell next to her books and journal. We wrote for another year and then I met my husband and moved to the UK. Though I wrote to her several times, I never heard from her again and I never did get back to see her. I have tried looking her up many times, but she must have been released because there's no record of her in the Virginia penitentiary records. I can't find her on social media either. Or maybe she met the man of her dreams and changed her name. But I keep trying, and wonder, sometimes, if she ever looks for me.

Rebecca Inmate #315***. Set free.

Prisoner. Dreamer. Parent. Person. Just like you and me.

The Music Man

I don't remember what first brought me to Reynolds Music on Castle Street. Was it a case for my daughter's first guitar or an enquiry for an instructor? Maybe one of several tin whistles purchased for me or the children, or was it the lovely Irish flute I sent back home as a birthday present for my niece?

What I do remember quite vividly, as I followed the curved and bumpy walkway, was how my arrival at the shop seemed symbolic of my current situation: the inner feeling of a descent toward an unseen cliff, an unavoidable drop off ~ with the store sign, acting as a figurative life-saving limb reaching out to break my fall. As a recent transplant from America to Northern Ireland crashing on sensory overload, here was finally something familiar- the black treble clef, one of the universal symbols of music recognizable anywhere in the world. And, for me personally, an old and dear friend.

Stepping across the threshold, I felt immediate warmth. The laughter of the employees, lighting set just right, the shimmering of the many instruments lining the walls and the enthusiastic attention of the owner, Mike Reynolds, made me forget for a moment, the bitter cold outside and the present concerns of my heart.

"Hello. It's a little wet outside." The men laughed.

"Just a little," I said, my coat glistening with water.

"Ah, that's not a local accent."

"No." I answered shyly never knowing if I would be welcome or rejected, "American. Pennsylvania."

"You're a long way from home. What brought you here?" Mike asked with genuine interest.

"Love." I smiled.

"Of course. It wasn't the weather!" We laughed again as the chill slowly faded away in the light of the welcoming shop.

After a few minutes of small talk, Mike showed me the different selections of woodwinds, brass and string instruments of which he was so fond and proud. On and on, they covered each nook and cranny, every spare inch of space. In addition to his obvious passion for all things musical, he was one of the kindest people I'd met so far. He was far too lively for my somber spirit to keep pace with, and yet I felt carried along as one does in the company of music.

I have been in many music stores, but Reynolds Music had a special magic in it, a singular generosity of spirit, that made me feel welcome, that it was okay to linger, to open my heart. It does not surprise me that Mike's passion is the baritone sax: warm, rich, strong and energetic. The store was alive with these elements, and something else I detected: an underlying feeling of camaraderie, inclusion-unity. I didn't feel like an outsider here.

The past months had fatigued me in mind, body and soul. Whether it was the roar of almost constant rain, the isolation of living in the country without the ability to drive, or missing family and friends, I often felt lonely. The settling in period of a new marriage of not only two personalities but two cultures, or the taxing confrontations by people who weren't as enthusiastic about my presence here as I was, contributed to a growing insecurity. Like cold waves out of the Atlantic, I felt more worn down with each day. Somewhere in the murky depths, I had stopped hearing the music of life and slipped into a monotone autopilot.

Survival mode happens to most of us at one time or another. Sometimes, it's through a traumatic event- a divorce, or a death of a loved one. At other times, it is not one situation, but many smaller experiences trampling upon us over a prolonged period. The same monotonous job that barely pays the bills, a long term illness that, while not terminal, stubbornly refuses to be cured or a friendship that keeps hitting the same painful bump in the road no matter how many ways you try to fix it.

All of this can build until one day the beauty of life- the tune we hear when we are filled with passion and purpose, in the story-line of a good movie, an evening of laughter and reminiscing with old friends, or falling in love- is suddenly lost and life seems dull, sad, even perhaps to the point of not worth living. I've met people who haven't heard a single note of life's music for a long time.

As I stood admiring a row of Irish flutes, I suddenly realized how people are a lot like instruments. We come in all shapes and sizes, different characters, different purposes. Some have the playful and mischievous nature of the tin whistle, others the dainty femininity of the flute. Men and women alike characterize the loud boom of the drum and the ability to set the pace and others embody both the strident and sweet tones of the violin. And yet an orchestra or a band plays in complete complementary harmony. Somehow, all the different resonances and styles weave together to make a beautiful sound, a joyful noise.

I have played clarinet since I was nine years of age in concert band, marching band, orchestra and even a special jazz ensemble and had a kinship with many of these instruments, their familiar timbres and personalities like old forgotten friends. Perhaps it is difficult to believe unless you are a music lover, but it felt as though the instruments recognized me too and immediately sensed something was wrong. Or perhaps they struck the chords of memory that reminded me of who I once was. The inner knotted cords loosened, and I smiled for the first time all day.

"Do you play?" Mike asked.

"Yes. I've played the clarinet since I was a child."

"You should come along to St. Eugene's Band."

"Oh, I haven't played in years. I wouldn't be any good. I don't even have a clarinet anymore."

"It'll come back to you. And I've got a clarinet you can borrow."

I agreed to give it a try and went one following Monday. I quickly discovered how sorely out of practice I was with more air escaping through the sides of my lips, like rapidly deflating balloons, than was making it though the clarinet. But what fun I had with such wonderful people every bit as welcoming as Mike had been at the shop. I learned that many of the members had never taken a lesson but had been self-taught later in life when they too realized something was missing, when they too had lost touch with life's music. I learned that St. Eugene's band, founded in 1894, was the first cross community band in Northern Ireland opening its arms to both Catholics and Protestants. This welcoming spirit was what I had felt in Mike's shop. I was humbled by my inclusion.

The joy of playing the clarinet again, my fingers palpating the familiar black holes, the silvery keys, hearing the resonant sound of my favorite woodwind, brought back so many memories playing in the orchestra and band with lifelong friends and of the sacred place music has held in my life. The changes and challenges of the past few months had been trying, but they could not alter my truest self. There is power in remembering.

Looking around the room at the other band members, and Mike preparing to conduct the next song, the joy in their faces was so apparent that the room seemed enlarged by it. And then it occurred to me that perhaps the reason we are able to get along in the band is because we understand our differences complement one another, together we are better- and, though we all have our own way of making music, we take our cues from the same man- The Music Man. The power of great leadership cannot be ignored.

Whether music for you is in an instrument, writing, caring for children, making flower arrangements, designing cars- find it and play! Play with an open heart so others, who have lost their song, can hear it again.

The Village Beauty

"Morning, beautiful" I say to myself in the bathroom mirror, eyes still sleepy, sun bursting in through the beveled window behind me. We don't get much sunshine here, so when it does come, it can feel a bit exposing.

I squint as yellow beams reflect in the mirror refracting my disheveled hair, twisted pajamas, and yesterday's runny make-up. It's a little like looking through a funky kaleidoscope.

"Morning, beautiful" I repeat with a wink. "Yeah, you. I'm talking to you - just as you are. You're beautiful and …I love you."

The moment feels a bit surreal, somewhat crazy. After years of feeling inadequate, this kindness is good, but weird. Many of us pass by mirrors first thing in the morning and spend the rest of the day using them to fix what we don't like, fashioning ourselves into what we do- the, sometimes, endless pruning and poking of the parts deemed less than adequate.

I've met men and women who struggle deeply with their physical appearance. Anorexia. Bulimia. Denying life. Purging sustenance. Often rooted in deeper, silenced pains. I spent years of my life living in shame. Not only for the mistakes I made, but for the bad person I believed I was. It's been a struggle all my life to believe God loves me - with no strings attached. Just as I am. Many times, I looked in the mirror and didn't like what I saw. Shame created a negative view of self, and of life, that had nothing to do with outward physique.

Sometimes, it's not so extreme, just simply the wrestling with growing older. When wrinkles and blemishes co-exist. That place between youth and old age where, for a time, the power seems to go out of us, and into everyone around us, until we find ourselves again. We aren't taught how hard it is to love, how long it will need to be sustained, and how to find that deep down resurrection joy and power that keeps us alive, keeps love flowing.

But I have been learning to live ~ and love ~ for some time now, and something feels different about today.

Like the shift in the seasons there is a shift in my soul. Something intangible, but so real, has changed. An almost imperceptible change like the first buds of spring, but undeniably in bloom. There is a resurrection coming, and its already here, in who I am as a daughter of God. I've been learning to see myself the way Abba sees me. It's taken me years of glimpses, peripheral revelations. This is an area I could battle all my life. But no doubt about it ~ the shift is here, and it is so sweet.

Brushing my hair, I recall a lunch several years ago with

my friend, Jamie. We met on the bus before I'd gotten my UK driving license. Jamie was born with Cerebral Palsy. She walked slowly and slurred her speech, but otherwise, her mind was sharp and her heart wide open. We were talking about friendships.

"You seem to have a good group of friends around you" I said to her taking a sip of coffee.

"They all have disabilities like me." She looked at me in a way I felt she was sizing me up. "I would love to have an able-bodied friend. Someone I can do things with." Was she asking me? I would be honored.

Jamie was a caretaker. Even though she was disabled, she was high functioning and often had to look after the others. She held a good job, and regularly travelled to Belfast to shop, and to businesses to speak about disability rights. I had met her other friends. They were good, kind people, but she was keenly aware of things they were not, and it had created longing.

"They're my friends. I love them. But...I need more." Her voice trailed off as her cheeks turned red and her speech slightly more strained. I reached out my hand to hers.

"It's okay, Jamie. I understand" I reassured her.

Taking one final look in the mirror, I finished getting ready and walked out the door for my appointment with one of the most beautiful women I know- inside and out. A woman who helps me be more. She does the waxing, shaping, and smoothing out of wrinkles mind, body and soul for our village tribe. She pampers our feet and our hearts. Every town has at least one woman who works her magic to transform, not just the outer beauty of the local women, but their inner beauty, too. We are not different from Jamie. We all need someone to bring out the treasure within.

Coming around the corner, I see Grainne, owner of The Village Beauty, leaning her small frame against the door. She looks across the street at the wedding party spilling from the chapel. Her long red hair glows in the sunlight like embers in a simmering fire. Arms gently folded across her black work dress, she gazes winsomely as the bride twirls and smiles under the same sun, yet in another world all her own.

Grainne embodies the power of true beauty: kindness for a stranger, hope for the broken hearted, lack of bitterness in a sweet spirit. She is a rare gem with always a kind word, an infectious smile, and a warm welcome bestowing grace. She holds a safe place for women to work out our long turbulent relationship with beauty. I am a better woman, wife and mother because of her friendship.

She waves and greets me.

"Hello, Nicole. How's things? How's the kids?" She genuinely wants to know.

"Sleeping in late. So, I snuck down to see you."

Her laughter is like the chimes at the door, a gentle ringing of acknowledgment.

"Oh, I know. My nieces are always up at the crack of dawn and my sisters would be the same." The lilt of her Irish accent dances playfully though the air. "Go on ahead into the room while I wash my hands."

I lie back on the table, the heaters radiating their warmth. The small room is cozy. A lingering scent of lavender oil relaxes and delights.

Grainne enters and swipes the moist cotton ball across my eyebrows. Only a quick waxing today but already I feel the week's stress melting away. The warm paraffin softens my whole face, seems to capture the thoughts in my mind and keep them from frenetically moving.

"Congratulations on your engagement. The pictures are beautiful."

She smiles and thanks me. We talk in low tones about the coming wedding and go over the details of how they met and when she knew he was the one for her. I have heard them before, but stories of falling in love bear repeating. She applies the sweet-smelling cream around my eye brows as we discuss those things only whispered in beauty treatment rooms, and hair salon chairs, where the gentle shaping of the physical draws out and remedies what is also tired, dry and split in the soul. Where women like Grainne, who know charm is deceptive and beauty fleeting, pluck out the deep splinters in the intimate places of their sisters so the eternal beauty can take root and flourish.

She holds the mirror for me to see. As always, her work is perfect. I smile.

"Morning, beautiful. Today is going to be a great day."

We laugh at my playfulness, but in the glowing light there is a sacred knowing. We all need an able person to help us see what we are not able to, at times. And from there it's a choice really. To see the beauty or not. To see our uniqueness or compare ourselves to others. To stay hidden in the shame of our past or come out into the open. To stay down, pushed down from failures or rise. To believe the lies spoken over us in darkness, or the truth of what God sees in us in the light. We were created to be the beautiful beloved. We just need others, sometimes, to help us see, to wipe away the debris, liberating the image of God within.

I believe and so I see. I see what I hope every person sees:

We are all the village beauty.

Into the Night

"For this God is our God for ever and ever; He will be our guide even to the end."
(PSALM 48:14)

The sanctuary of the small country church glowed with the gentle, dancing light of ivory candles. Crimson holly berries sprung from the cascading evergreens adorning the deep window sills. Beyond the glass the dark winter night was quiet and still. Families, packed shoulder to shoulder in the wooden pews, exuded a mixture of contentment and anticipation. It was a characteristic Christmas Eve service whose yearly ritual of song and story opened the doorway into the season's gifts of joy and wonder.

As the little kids' nativity play ended, and they exited the stage, we were introduced to our guest speaker, a local woman who would be sharing her story with us. I was only ten years old, yet already an enthusiastic writer, and I enjoyed hearing about people's lives. Their experiences fascinated me, especially if I could eavesdrop on conversations I wasn't supposed to hear.

But, truthfully, church testimonies often bored me. They seemed too contrived, not part of real life at all, and I was looking forward to it all being over so we could go home and open our Christmas Eve gifts. However, the woman at the pulpit, whose name I have long forgotten, was going to tell a story like I had never heard before.

I would remember it every Christmas for the rest of my life.

She was a pretty, petite woman with wispy brown hair and a sweet voice. At first, she read carefully from the concise sentences she had written on a few pieces of paper. As she gained confidence, she increasingly met our gaze in the softly lit sanctuary, and we became intimate companions as the details of her life unfolded.

She and her husband had married young and happy. They had two beautiful daughters and she was a stay-at-home Mom while he worked to provide for the family. Her voice lilted and cracked as she spoke of her children whom she obviously loved very much. She told us a little about their life, where they lived, their hopes and dreams - until finally she faltered, and then stopped all together.

The room grew silent in the expectant pause, the candles flickered waiting patiently, yet quietly urging her on. A foreboding sadness entered my heart.

She could not remember when the beatings started or why. At first, it was hard - no, impossible - to understand what was happening. She took the abuse, coping as best she could, desperately searching for answers to her husband's altered personality. She protected their daughters from the worst of it by sending them to friends and relatives when things became unbearable. When she could take no more, she prayed and asked God to show her a way to safety. Here she stopped and boldly looked down at her now teenage girls.

"Your Daddy loves you so much and so do I. And I still love your Dad, and so does God."

Her words rang with hope and conviction. She faced the congregation again.

"I'm not telling this story to shame or hurt him, but to tell of God's guidance and grace in the real circumstances of our lives. Secular society often scoffs at God, and the church does not like to acknowledge abuse. But abuse is real, and God is there and an ever-present help in it."

I looked around at the faces I could see from where I sat next to my Mom and Nana. Expressions of compassion and sorrow formed their countenances glowing in the soft light of the sanctuary. A few shifted in their seats and looked away. Even as a child it was not hard to understand this gentle woman's story was making some people uncomfortable. Long-standing church members, and those who had come only to see their children play shepherds and angels or listen to Christmas carols, had been confronted with the hard reality of abuse. Others hung on her every word. It struck me that this was exactly how it should be. In the middle of these hard things were what Jesus was born into, what He lived through. What He came to earth for. The room seemed to swell with the thought of it, until I almost expected Jesus to walk through the door. She bravely continued.

"After I prayed, God began moving. People came into my life that I could talk to, people that could help me. The Holy Spirit told me what to pack and where to hide my suitcase so my husband would not find it. Then the night came, the Holy Spirit woke me up and told me to call my contact. My husband stayed asleep while I took the suitcase, and the girls, and snuck out of the house where a car was waiting, and we were taken to safety."

She continued marveling over all the ways God had provided for them. Incapable of comprehending the full gravity of the situation, I still understood something both terrible and miraculous had happened in this woman's life.

Circumstances had brought her bitter pain, disappointment, and the unwanted heartache and burden of a broken family, but this was not the end of the story. In fact, it wasn't even her main focus. God was alive and present in her tragedy and had come to rescue her. Her story, as dangerous and sad as it was, was also a beautiful journey, a modern-day Christmas story of fragile human beings stepping out into the night of the unknown to follow Jesus to freedom.

In no way do I wish to minimize or romanticize domestic violence and neither did she. Her family's pain was palpable. The one who should have brought protection and security instead wreaked harm and havoc upon three defenseless people. Abuse is heartbreaking reality suffered by women, children, and men, too.

What made her story so miraculous was her focus, not on the abuse, but on God's faithfulness in leading her and her daughters to safety. The extraordinary events were much like the way He led Joseph and Mary to the stable just in time for Jesus' birth. He brought provision through the Wise Men, and then gave them a dream telling them to go home another way and not tell Herod where the baby Jesus was. God also gave Joseph a dream to escape to Egypt so Herod could not find them. God's guidance in her escape from abuse added new facet of redemption to the birth of the babe in the manger, probably not the redemption her bride's heart would have chosen, but the one a perfect, loving God prepared for her because He knew the road that lay ahead. I looked up at my Nana. Though pain was etched into her features, her eyes shone with that light they always did whenever she spoke about Jesus.

In that moment I understood God's voice was not just for people in the Bible, for the past. It was for us- for now.

"I love my husband so much. I want the same things for him that God gave to me and the girls: a way of escape from his torment. Peace. Joy. These things are available to all of us who believe in Jesus, who came to this earth all those years ago to be with us, our Emmanuel. Today, He is still with us and He wants to be in every area of our lives. If we'll let Him. He's the Christmas gift that keeps on giving." She laughed and folded her papers. "Thank you for listening to me tonight."

I watched as she stepped down and took her seat in the pew. Her daughters cuddled into her as she put her arm securely around them. I wondered what their Christmas would be like and where her husband was now, and what he would think if he had heard her speak tonight. I wondered, too, at the strange feeling of love I felt toward a man I didn't know, and the keen hope residing in my heart that her husband would one day turn to Jesus and maybe be able to return to his family. Candles were passed around and lit as if in united affirmation of her powerful, heartfelt story of Christ, the light of the word shining in the dark. We sang the last carol of the evening, Silent Night, which seemed to me, even more solemn and brighter than usual.

As Christmas comes around each year, I pause and reflect on that service, the woman and her family, their story. When the singing falls silent, the children are asleep, and the house quiet, I read the Christmas story and think of what God did in the birth of Jesus. Born in the lowest of places, in hard circumstances, singing His song "You are not alone. You and your circumstances won't chase me away. This is what I was born for." God sent His Son to us, The Light that will never go out.

What I see most clearly, what gives me hope, is that the light of Christ shines for every one of us, and in that light is our true identity. In the addict, a grandfather. The homeless, a messenger. In a criminal, a hero. In a band leader, His unity. In a wanderer, His story. And in you, dear reader, a son, a daughter, His dream.

We are all His Somebody.

Printed in Great Britain
by Amazon

51931784R00051

AQUATINTS

New Poems

2012 - 2015

Peter Dale

THE MINILITH PRESS

Published in 2015 by
The Minilith Press
11 Heol Y Gors
Whitchurch
Cardiff, CF14 1HF

© Peter Dale 2015

Peter Dale has asserted his right under the Copyright, Design and Patents Act, 1988 to be identified as the author of this work.

ISBN: 978-0-9929875-4-1

British Library Cataloguing in Publication Data
A catalogue record of this book is available from the British Library.

All rights reserved. Except for purposes of review no part of this book may be reproduced, stored in a retrieval system or transmitted in any means without the express permission of the the publisher.

Printed and bound in Cardiff
by Abbey Book Binding and Printing Ltd, Gabalfa, Cardiff, CF14 3AY.

Acknowledgements

Some of these poems have appeared in *Acumen, Agenda, New Poetry Quarterly* and the booklet *Fathoming Earth*, published by The Minilith Press, Cardiff.

'Mary's Carol' has been set to music by Antony le Fleming (Good Music) for choral performance, by Michael Linton (USA) and by Paul Pott published in *The Ivy and Holly*, OUP. A setting of 'Mary's Lullaby' by Humphrey Clucas is published by Animus.

The quotation in 'About the Author' is used by permission of R.V. Bailey from her review of *Diffractions*, in *Acumen*, 75, 2013.

Cover: 'Standing Stones' is an original etching and aquatint by Janet Clucas, © 2015

The Minilith Press Logo is designed by Nick Davies.

Memories gather poignancy like dust.
                Robert Goddard: *Found Wanting*

IN MEMORIAM

PIERS DALE 1964–2013

Sadly now,
when our phone rings at your unearthly hours,
it won't be you, unless, don't tell us how,
you manage to good-wink the celestial powers.

AQUATINTS

CONTENTS

IN LIVING MEMORY
   Wild Goose Chase   17
   Grace Notes   19
   Retroscope   20
   Piece-Meal   21
   Living Memory   23
   Whispering Galleries   25
   Reflective Poet   27
   Talking the Walk   28
   Reaches   27
   Sorting old Photographs   30
   Charity Shop   32
   Annual   33
   Nonsuch Park and Easter Island   38

BEES IN BONNETS: SONNETS
   Exile   39
   The Hurlers   40
   The Compass Rose   41
   The Sitter Thinks   42
   Labradorescence   43
   Dream Team   44
   Transcription   45
   Gap Years   46
   Pageants   47
   The Small Hours   48
   1918-1939   49
   Unending Song   50
   Alto Rhapsody   51

NIGHT-CAPS

Insomniac Lullaby	53
Winter Lullaby	54
Lullaby: White-Out	56
Largo Lullaby	57
Mary's Carol	58
Mary's Lullaby	59

ILL-ASSORTED SONGS

The Valley	61
Seen but not Heard	62
Sing Along	63
Holding Operation	64

FOUR BY FOURS

Old Poets Shelved	65
Reflection	65
Walk	65
Futures	66
Privateers	66
Boots	66
Towards Even-Tide	66

FLASH POINTS

Short Sight	67
Spate	67
Early Morning	67
Dainty Ankles	67
Gusts	68
Light Dawning	68
Dead Set	68

Cross Purposes	68
Mud	68
Seasonal Dither	69
Rain-Spotting	69
Side-Light	69

LIKELY TALES

Ballad of the Unrepentant Thief	71
Sprat to Catch a Mackerel	74
The Dowser	76

ENVOI

The Rods: Closure and Disclosure	81

ABOUT THE AUTHOR	82

IN LIVING MEMORY

WILD GOOSE CHASE

A short cut, we called it The Slip:
a bit of road, left to an earth path,
then fork right to 'this-and-that' shop';
left to fire-station. Stay right for park.

Ways where the grown-ups never went.
They said because of all that dirt.
At the road end were the three quaint
cottages of eighteen-something date.

We knew: they were scared of the geese
outside one cottage, free to roam.
That wasn't hard for kids to guess.
They scared us too – and made us scram.

Great rolling chests like longboat sails,
their racket worse than guard dogs. We dared
each other past them, courageous souls
we were. The hazards we endured:

the towpath swans that blocked the way;
the sewer pipe for river bridge,
leapfrogged along – or worse, the weir
and teeter barefoot along the edge.

'Not me she saw, mum. It wasn't me.'
You soak up gramper's tales, imagine
he's eighteen-something, suspect you may
have no such fun – the jammy urchin.

It wasn't me; not special, no way;
it was everyone's: the slips, the geese,
the makeshift bridges – everywhere.

Just listen to the silly old goose.

GRACE NOTES

We were together there. We were together then.
You were with me. You *were*. I was with you. We *were*.
Yet neither of us risks to venture a when or where
for fear that neither could authenticate – one thing.

We saw in each other's eyes. An under-cliff, it was.
The gulls, silver to sunward, seaward, gliding, side-
slipping down the thermals till lazily they soared.
Slight as the mussel shell's, the lines of dark-blue waves.

Eye-shadow over your lids, the profile of their under-wings.
I mentioned it. Laughing at me, you side-slipped your head.
Well, didn't you? Called the whereabouts our open hide?
We're getting it together. Both could fix where we were once.

Gulls wheeled in spirals, martins darted over drying sands.
Was it the first of the lasts of all that? Or last of the firsts?
– Ubiquitous gulls, urban gulls at their land-fill feasts.

One love long lost, one call forever crying since …

RETROSCOPE

They're lively, going into hall to dine,
and after to some do:
suits, off-the-shoulder ball-gowns, slipping shawls.
Too cold for that.
But they don't know it, two and two
– yet seem to know where they are at.

They gather in the festal light:
dance-music, friends, see and be seen,
and ring changes on slight and sleight.
They move as if assured they see
what is to come …
                      till it has been.
They talk too loud – for victory.

It was always too loud.
The unwatched eye of an ill-chosen future
careers across their past as they stroll by,
dwindling into the lurking years.

PIECE-MEAL
   For William Bedford

The blazing sun
chipping scalene notches of matching shadow
into the wall-corner beyond you, pseudo
saw-teeth – not from your perch to be seen.

What old gaffers.
Friends since the nine-days' wonder of youth,
we shuffle our share of life-times back and forth,
sardonic, wry, our so-called get-togethers.

Old friend, we're lost.
Do *you* guess why, what, who *I* misremember:
words, details, names? Me ditto you ... penumbra
from deeds and gatherings dematerialized?

And the scarp side –
if like last time – grey shades behind my back.
You might be noting grades of black. – Its bulk
fray-edged with splintered light, you'd said.

But worse, my friend,
the whys and wherefores of detail we record:
what gathers round the fragments, words, recalled?
How do they tally? What, who have we framed?

Pieces we hold,
scuffed jigsaw bits we'll force to click and match
– or keep some back? Focus, close-ups we smudge,
fake insets we patch up, fix and hoard.

Old friend, they're lost,
our dead friends, in these meetings: smithereens
of ours and other minds, rag stone of runes;
significance, secrets, grafitied, lapsed.

Lacunae, memos, quirks, sayings:
betrayal, it feels, to broach and bodge them –
more like ours than time's.
A breach in trust,
deafly their absent presence murmurs.

LIVING MEMORY
For Helen Melody

Friends and contemporaries, too early dead,
you sidle from the bookshelves to appear
clamouring mutely: *Still here; do you hear?*
– I cannot tell what it is you would have said.

I would speak for you, ghost ventriloquy,
yet now your lived-in voices blur and merge
in murmurs, half-heard rhythms that converge.
– It is your silence speaks to me, of me.

I would speak in hope our words will last.
We've not inscribed our say in slow stone;
spoke gist, hint, feint, shade, nuance, undertone
– fleeting, if no ears hang on seed broadcast.

And some there be that have no memorial.

Driven when young, we meant to make our own:
our living words to stand in flesh and bone,
mouthfuls of air – like rock perennial.

Such as found out musical tunes
and recited verses in writing ...

Oceans have come
and gone. In network waves new records hum:
quartz crystal sand-grains drift in shifting dunes.

WHISPERING GALLERIES

You write for just a few people
   in hope one day they'll understand:
close friends who'd not accept a purple
     passage nor anything too grand;

something like a whisper in the night
   of lover, conscience, friend, stray ghost,
or lines some friend takes as a note,
   and have the meaning heard by most.

Over slow years some words are heard
   by old and recent friends that come and go,
though notes are things few people hoard.
   Yet who, when, where you may not know.

It seems a case of Chinese whispers.
   I catch them first, a muted gist,
and hope to pass them on, as aspens
     whisper the breeze to those who listen.

Lines come and go like friends and neighbours,
   as laden ships that pass in the night,
each bound for various, unknown harbours,
    Lundy, Cromarty, Dogger, Wight.

My days were taken with the lure of words,
    as daffodils take the winds of March
with beauty: gone with scant rewards,
    mouthfuls of air that weighed too much.

REFLECTIVE POET

He looked in the mirror where he saw a face
the god Apollo featured as his gift
and what he saw he liked, physique and eyes
that would have drawn Narcissus from the pool
to clasp his love where not a breath of air
could ripple across the surface of his gaze.

The mirror tried outstaring him. Glass fixed
his gaze and what returned its scrutiny
was the god's child and gurning human brat.
Medusan, it had frozen the clever child
who wished his whims and fads were cut in stone
that wouldn't break the mirror's dwindled world.

He took his pocket mirror from its case,
half-turned and smiled in it from his odd angle
to show the pier-glass what it had to see:
infinite regression of a self-reflective form.
He saw his portrait dwindling in the distance
into a trivial infinitesimality.

TALKING THE WALK

It was a dream and not a dream:
my oldest friend, respected most,
you, striding off through dark woods.
And I, not there, called to your back,
unheard or heeded. I wondered why,
when it might be, feared when it was.

We often meet to have a drink
and talk about what drives us on,
and each can often second guess
the other's take on what is what.
– You, walking off through the dark woods
where one of us becomes a ghost.

A ghost won't haunt another ghost.
Whose shade casts dread on our old haunts?
Whose words and hours blown through a sieve?
The vacant spirit can't be laid.
Old friend, have you vanished now?
– Here I go, still talking to myself.

REACHES

Now we have come to live in this crescent of hills
in Wales beside the Severn shore
I see more sky than heretofore
when just a boy in watery Surrey: rills,
bourns, Thames, canals, the mill-pond's sky, the lakes';
aloft, the long clouds like speedboat wakes.

Slate slab nimbus, edged with filaments of sun;
flat-bottom cumulus toppling; row
on row of cirrus furrows like driven snow;
skies still or dithery; flocks of wool at the run;
the gripping silence of suspense till the storm raves
with the craquelure of lightning sizzling to the waves.

All here; still there; but the sea was in the sky:
wide reaches with sun-gold clouds for shores;
meandering estuaries through purple moors;
white horses of cloud; steamer trails on high.
Oh, such is childhood after the event
and landing here is just the way things went.

SORTING OLD PHOTOGRAPHS

Who took this formal snap?
    What did they think to capture:
three brothers, biggy in the middle;
    left, the youngest big kid;
right, the in-between seems highbrow,
    leaning further to the right
with ironic, side-glance eye,
    his figure rather slight.

But biggy is a standing stone,
    missing his circle cronies.
He clearly thinks he's leader.
    His brothers see no need.
Three boys in three moments
    of contiguous times tri-forking:
highbrow, nose like a gnomon,
    reluctant, showing awkward.

Why and how posed the photo?
    Is this what the camera focused
through someone's humorous eye:
    monolith, minilith, highbrow?
Have I restored the picture clearly
    or forged historical record?
Is deep grief printed here,
    each second, by second, by second?

No pictures in the album
    of three at play and pally;
few other family snaps
    and none with useful captions.
Why do I keep this leftover,
    discarding all the rest?
(Both acts feel acts of theft.)
    Obsessed by the possessed?

But what and why first cherished
    no after-comer inherits,
nor sees just what I've seen,
    poor repository of mismeanings:
three boys, no trio together.
    We have no second sight
to see their inner weather:
    each gaze a changing light.

CHARITY SHOP

Jewellery, locked in a glazed stand,
and costume jewellery, attractive some of it,
once stylish, years before we both were born.
No problems over whether it would fit.
Yet who would want to wear it second-hand,
a stranger's finery, already worn?
Then we remember clearing house and home,
a mass of jewellery, ear-rings to tiara comb.

Some costume. Most antiques and heirlooms,
some youthful wit, some ostentatious, vain.
You never saw her wear much of it, though:
left-over hopes, lapsed wishes, castles in Spain;
balls, dances, parties, dinners in ritzy rooms.
Wrong stones, vibes someone else might find her style;
another conjure cast-off gems to beguile.

ANNUAL

CONCERT

Beyond the east window,
restored with clear glass,
a bare tree branches up
its fan vaulting
on the Feast of Christmas.

IF WINTER COMES ...

Leafless, a dead tree
fronts the flowering cherry
back-lit by morning sun,
– a stained glass window
glazed with snow.

SPRING WATCH

The fresh leaves of the young aspen
in the wayward breeze
shuffle and nudge this way and that,
jostling in a crowd to see
which side the spectacle will be.

HOME RUN

Street of unpaved footpaths, bourn that floods,
no matter where you are,
you sidle past the old house every day,
the lane where pea-shooter hawthorn buds.
It's long distant; you have gone far.
But there it is. Out of your way.

SWANS

Swans,
cumulus separating and gathering
on a reflected summer;
more, under the arches of trees,
feeding, rear up, heads under water,
their bodies
like the glass white-flame shades on lamps
in a cool, wayside church.

EVERGREEN MUSAK

Piped music,
some vintage romantic love-song.
The old girl,
lost in her memories, sings along.
She can't keep time.
More's the pity.

Song that any one of us could hum.

LAMENT

Coppery, orange, amber,
the leaves must fall
as tears do.

Ah, leaves, go slowly, slowly,
or you will cover her grave
too soon.

Oh, when none or few …

AUTUMN MISTS

Low cloud topping the hills,
like slow-motion storm breakers,
bursting over in spray.

The river
with its plaited ropes of silt-brown flow
undercuts the bank,
the grass overhang like tousled foreheads of kids.
Silt augments the inner bend till ...

Ancestral precipitate.
We shall not see the ox-bow lake.

LOGIC

The faultless logic of snow:
it notes each horizontal,
each level, ledge or lintel
and settles on them now ...

Smooth white copings slip
from post and wall and sill;
the plants make rings of soil
stretch oval, overlap.

But, there, look, still a patch
of plump and frozen plush,
clean white beneath that bush,
maintains its stubborn pitch.

The eye banks on that sight
for days to hold its own,
overlooked, opposite …
Another leftover gone.

*

NONSUCH PARK; EASTER ISLAND

Hardwood's the best all-weather timber.
Well made with brass memorial plaques,
the headstone benches stare at winter
in this and a thousand parks.

New benches, built to thwart the vandals,
glint their names across the grass.
More seats than seated in green rectangles
wait for winter to pass.

They watch for Primavera, the goddess,
her equable spring – or Eastertide.
– Villages by the logged rain-forest
dregs in the mud-slide.

BEES IN BONNETS: SONNETS

Note: the following two sonnets are from an unpublished novel and written in character.

EXILE

My lovely country is a land-locked realm.
The mountains thwart the child imagining seas,
the troughs of those vast breakers, evergreen trees,
no pen nor print could ever overwhelm.

Now captious Ahab's bearing holds the helm,
the land is ice-bound, white horses topped with snow.
Snow-bodies freeze on floes that do not flow.
Banned is my language – uttered still, though seldom.

Its culture threads back past paper, birch plaque, vellum.
I will not speak Ahabic; the mother tongue
is mine, and mine its voice: it must be sung.
Mobius dicta I am, and most unwelcome.

An exile in a land unspeakable,
I watch, I warn; my beat is littoral.

THE HURLERS

The Hurlers are three Bronze Age stone circles near the famous Cheese Wring Megaliths, in Cornwall. Somewhat damaged and ruinous, they are still impressive, although their name is less so, based on a mediaeval Christian legend that they represent teams of men petrified for the sin of playing the Celtic game of hurling on the Sabbath.

I cannot answer your decree, outlanders.
I do not jaw the jargon that you bark.
You perpetrate such howlers, alien blunders.
My speech is not according to your book.

I know your euphemisms through loud-hailers
In every would-be rule you up and utter.
Try speaking to the moors, command The Hurlers.
We hold the inward; they the granite outer.

Our language, our culture, raised that monument
And thousands like it; only in foolish legends
Can they be moved – by night and devilish command,
Steadfast strong-holders, unbudged by legions.

Our tongue is whispering. Hark, a knifing draught.
Our megaliths mark your star-fall. You're cast adrift.

THE COMPASS ROSE

The sunlight, look, reflects off the east cliff
and tints the western bluff that rosé pink.
We have our bearings, think we know what's what,
so don't look north, as if the sun sets there.
– Or is it rises? Someone's postcards, snaps
of what appears could easily deceive
a stranger to believe both cliffs are pink;
sunset, or rise perhaps, to north to us.

– We should have named the back. Where was this place?
Dozens there must be like it, facing north.
– It might have been south-facing, even west,
dozens more. Limestone cuts the count at least.
It could have faced due east, rose-fingered dawn.
We've lost our bearings. Now we're strangers there.

THE SITTER THINKS
I.m. Tamasin Cole

This is not my moment. You think it's yours.
You want to fix it by your eye and hand,
to capture me on canvas, world without end.
No moment, me. I am momentum, hours,
days, years. So dash around and dash your paint
about in agitation. My eye holds yours.
Don't try to give me any of your airs.
A cleavage drift, look, spins your compass point.

Who shall remember this for years to come?
You want me to. I'd need a replica.
Cheap enough these days. Yet, you'd claim,
it couldn't do justice to your moniker.

– I'll tuck in mind you dashing round my calm.
I'll nudge my skirt ajar, ham silly cow.

LABRADORESCENCE
 For Kit Yee Wong

A fragment of labradorite, purchased where?
A comfortable handful or piece to display,
palm-size, edges natural, face polished smooth.
In changing lights of day and night it gives:
a small bay, cliff enclosed, its scythe of sand,
over-arched by wind-warped saplings, larger boughs;
or creek, moon-bright; the lateral flame of a stream;
or tide of amber sunrise – all from cliff height.

Places we've seen? Or does it inculcate
scenes where neither it nor we have been?
In other hands and angles, different sights?
Our haven cliff – one day we'll find the place
– or, unaware, project it on some likely bay
with this uncanny sense of déjà vu.

DREAM TEAM

How to retaliate against a dream?
– In late teens we'd parted by mutual drift,
she churchward, I to the scientific extreme,
changed localities and partners in the shift.
We crossed again when years had done their worst.
I'd not looked back from wizen face, grey head;
library spectacle frames, she'd spotted first,
both dragged by family bonds to streets we'd fled.

Years on, you show up in a summer dream:
three kids pre-teen at play with you, prime wife.
You gloat full-on, the cat that stole the cream,
disporting the fulfilment in your life.
A dream, address unknown – how to respond?
Beam a dark matter smirk from the back of beyond?

TRANSCRIPTION

Why do this, your voice over a decade dead,
transcribing this now old, long-misboxed tape,
shop-talk of how and why we did as we did,
the life in words? – And such a chore to type.

Your voice so quiet and by turns succinct
and hesitant, obscured by restaurant din.
Your wine-list check for halves. – We'd always sunk
another whole bottle. … Just a page done.

I cannot type your voice, the traits of tone,
and your inflexional glances. So few are left,
dear friend, who heard you, who could return
cold print to voice over. Books took our life.

We blued our days in words – on living words,
we thought, and it has come to this: is – was.

GAP YEARS
   I. m. Dr John Cobb

John, seeker of strange pubs there was,
compassionate with all but routine day,
became a doctor; 'to avoid most whites'
went to Uganda as if it were a dare.

And always coming back, he said he was.
Traced me working up north one blue moon,
bringing a crate of beer. ... But it cuts both ways.
Rare meetings, hey-days left circling in mind.

Occasional encounters that I took for life.
Three fields, a lane, tree-lined, a trellis fence;
More practice needed for age and loneliness.
You are so many, John, so many friends.
Not so. A last time you traced our new address.
We vaporised the gap years like dry ice.

PAGEANTS

Familiar figures, not now known to me,
sauntering through the dusken semi-dream
of waxing dawn like leaves upon a stream;
familiar features, encroached by anonymity,
and which were friends, which foes with whom, wiped free,
and no great shakes, though once thought so.
My nameless face, most likely, jetsam in the flow
of their pre-waking dreams – and all at sea.

Rivalries, friendships, matched and ill-matched loves,
ah, unweathered faces, no i.o.u.s;
rivals who spurred or thwarted, friends who baulked –
'and under him my genius is rebuked...'
intended acts or not, both mine and yours.
Names, worn and torn, are fraying from our lives.

THE SMALL HOURS

I have been making dates to meet friends dead.
in our old stamping grounds before they left,
that restaurant, English cooking at its best,
but they're much less reasonable since they went
and want the meeting point much nearer them.
Well past their spans, and my three score and ten,
infirm, infirm, I haven't got the legs
to cross the town by night to suit their ends.

Mad. What are you saying? In your dreams.

But in your sleep of death no dreams may come.
I am the meeting point, your radial hub.
One of few left and not so far afield.
There's one date your way that we each must keep –
a time, as never before, none of us meet.

1918–1939

Rank, name, regiment, numbers, dates:
Private R L Corben, R.E.M.E.1920-43.
– Uniform stone, and bone it commemorates,
someone known only to the War Graves Cemetery.
Len Corben was never one for the formal slot.
His folk never visited this foreign spot.

Family and friends knew him as Jet Sam.
Behind his back and hers, Floss Sam his wife.
His boy enjoyed the name Sam Son or Sam Wham.
Family and friends are now as dead.
The legend of this stone they'd left unread.

As with the prehistoric lines of megaliths
at Carnac, future times will weave their myths.

UNENDING SONG

Lena, I visited the grounds of the dead
to find you. You weren't there. How could you be?
I never got back. Your billet is my head.
How could I? *Your pigeon. Don't look to me.*

What ways are there to live and not to christen
death in the minds of loved and loving ones?
Your curt injunctions help: *I speak; you listen.*
– Lena, Leena, Leeena! Last of your sons,

croupy grampus, one of God's awkward ones,
I can call you that now, Leeena! See if I care.
*You'll get the back of my hand, my lad. There,
rings and all!*
            Words. ... But that woman's voice,
the other you, songs not needing words. No choice
you left me ... You did not stay to heard your son's.

ALTO RHAPSODY

Her music, she had a lovely alto voice
but never had a chance of rhapsody.
She sang west Wiltshire tunes, the melancholy
of villagers who'd to choose what was no choice.

Always the low registers in the war,
as if high would draw the bombers overhead.
Two hours of daylight saving, and late to bed,
I'd hear her melodies come through the floor.

Her song without words, I hear it still,
breaking in fragments through any floor or wall,
not subject to the hour or to the will,
those registers that never rose to fall.

How shall I learn her words of endless song?
They murmur their largo my whole life long.

NIGHTCAPS

INSOMNIAC LULLABY

I would compose myself to sleep.
    No lie of the hands leads to rest.
The lengthened shadows blend and creep;
    dark floats the light up in the west.

I would compose myself to sleep.
    My hands cannot lay hold of rest.
Sweet dream, the impenetrable keep
    that circling thoughts night long invest.

The world has lost its perfect dark.
    I would compose myself to sleep.
Oh, hands, lie still like fallen bark.
    If the dreams came they would weep.

WINTER LULLABY

The sandman is coming,
    drowsy one,
from sea-sides of summer
    and warm sun.

He'll sprinkle dream magic
    round your head.
You'll see his bright pageants
    snug in bed.

Your toys lie so idle
    after play.
His dream-time will tidy
    all away.

With dream-dust he'll trickle
    on your lids
green pictures of picnics,
    games for kids.

You nestle in pillows,
    dreamy one,
and sleep in the stillness.
    Day is done.

The snowman is coming,
    Christmas lights.
And soon it's the summer,
    shorter nights.

So snuggle up tight, then,
    cosy one.
The moon is your night-light.
    Dream up fun.

LULLABY: WHITE-OUT
For Eleanor

She sleeps as quiet as the falling snow,
    levelling over the uneven ground,
as soundless as the field-mouse lying low,
    as silent as the owl skims piece and pound.

She sleeps as soundless as the owl flies,
    searching the rides and meadows to and fro,
as silent as the field-mouse seals its eyes,
    beneath the wavering flakes of settling snow.

A dream beneath her eyelids shyly slides,
    soundlessly as the field-mouse seals its eyes,
as secret as the starving owl glides,
    as seamless as the land in snow's disguise.

Yet when she wakens to the winter light
    does she conceal the dream that slipped through sleep?
Or does the dream hide who she is from sight,
    and passive as the snow the silence keep?

She sleeps as settled as the hushful snow,
    levelling over the uneven ground
as silent as the field-mouse lying low,
    as secret as the wings that make no sound.

LARGO LULLABY

The long, diminuendo, largo twilight
    promises pianissimo night,
though stars, staccato in the skylight,
    pepper the mind's eye with light.

Some stars, staccato in the twilight,
    will blaze to black holes of night.
Our little snapshot in the skylight
    blinkers us from imploded light.

Low, diminuendo, largo twilight
    leads us into the still night.
The stars, staccato, the moon's highlight,
    look lullabies to finite sight.

MARY'S CAROL

Why do you give the baby gold?
The guiding star foretold a king.
A little child shall lead you, bring
   No metal rich and cold.

Who brings my boy this frankincense?
The star foretold a priestly role.
A little child shall save your soul,
   Not gifts of great expense.

What is this myrrh? What do you see?
The star foretold a bitter cup.
'And I if I be lifted up
   Shall draw all men to me.'

A child shall lead you from tonight.
   The angel heralded his birth.
Our Saviour born to save the earth,
   Our Way, our Truth, our Light.

Three gifts that far outweigh all gold
   And gifts like frankincense and myrrh.
Sleep, child, my little comforter,
   That no star has foretold.

MARY'S LULLABY

    A silence where the angels sang
        And all the shepherds gone away.
    Oh now I feel the sharpest pang.
        What shall I pray?

    Sleep, little one, you go to sleep
        And do not hear the things I say
    That I must ponder long and keep
        Hidden away.

    A mother guards you, sleepy head.
        She does not want to see one thorn.
    Dream sweetly in your straw-made bed,
        Oh, my first born.

    A mother tucks your cold hands in
        And marvels at their tiny nails.
    How shall they bear the dark world's sin?
        My heart fails.

    My little lamb, I'll take you up
        And lull you in my swaying arms.
    Tonight there is no bitter cup,
        No crowds, no palms.

I must not and I must believe.
    It's winter; ivy clings like love.
I must not grieve and yet I grieve
    For God above.

Sleep, little one, now safely sleep.
    You must not hear the things I say,
Words I must ponder long and keep
    Hidden away.

ILL-ASSORTED SONGS

THE VALLEY

In the valley of the lilies long ago
    you walked with me those days that outlast years.
The rain-weighed branches sprinkled all below
    with glistening drops that were not tears.

While the season of the lilies comes and goes
    I walk along those days that haunt the year,
lilies that have to pass as your frail ghost
    beside the willows' long green weir.

Yet the willows do not weep; the river's course
    erodes the valley with its flood and flow.
The lilies have no passion, no remorse.
    What could a shade from Lethe know?

SEEN BUT NOT HEARD
For Owen

No Viking warlord, Saxon chief,
    my mother's brother – dead.
How real was all that gold-hoard grief
    that round the warriors spread?

He'd gone when I was nowhere near.
    They would not let me be.
Rock solid silence boxed my ear.
    They would not talk round me.

I hurled big stones into the bourn;
    rings bobbed about the flow,
rough flints and pebbles water-worn;
    too many stones to throw.

I launched my treasured model boat
    far out across the bourn.
I watched it roll and downstream float –
    and doubly then could mourn.

SING ALONG

She quavers her predicted song
    in any unpredictable night.
I cannot, will not sing along.
    That *vox humana*'s no delight.

She quavers her *da capo* airs,
    appropriating any dream.
These sound-bites now are all she dares.
    –Try con *amore* on my theme.

In haunting songs you come and go
    where memory inverts the tune.
Clear out and ham another show
    far off beneath a bluer moon.

HOLDING OPERATION

The stitches are itching,
the aches are a pain,
the muscles keep twitching,
the blood-flow's in vain.

The eyesight's deceptive,
the hearing is hard,
the brain's not receptive,
the joints are jarred.

We're falling back
on every front.
We must attack
as a last stunt.

FOUR BY FOURS

OLD POETS SHELVED

A poem's a word for which we had no other word.
In it we speak ourselves
so that, when long interred,
the miniatures of spirits shift about the shelves.

REFLECTION

Yes, you've the figure, features made to stun.
Vanity has an audience of one –
and that, you see,
is never me.

WALK

Summer. I strolled into a country church
and sat down to savour the cool, still air.
Cold-calling, I was left there in the lurch.
Defunct the intercom; they called it prayer.

FUTURES

You never daydreamed in the womb
of what a life to come might be.
Why speculate beyond the tomb
on tediums of eternity?

PRIVATEERS

We set out on our writing lives together,
And, young, we both went at it hell for leather,
then sailed off, charting seas of inner weather.
Now, nearing landfall, we're at the end of our tether.

BOOTS

One of the unexpected fruits
   of changing into winter boots
is that you do not have to bend so low
   to tie the laces up and go.

TOWARDS EVEN-TIDE

Bridge railings reflect on
and shadow the river.
The jumper breaks all.

FLASH-POINTS

SHORT SIGHT

Thunderous flight of swans, low
over the bridge,
crash-lands. From wet to dry. Why?

SPATE

Flint flakes of sun on the flow
erode footings
of the old stone-arched bridge.

EARLY MORNING

Sun-lit wet kingfisher,
the brook's pristine, split second jewel.
Far too wordy.

DAINTY ANKLES

Squirrel nest-raiding their tree.
A pair of black-birds peck his ankles.
Flight.

GUSTS

Each time gusts sway the chrysanths
the bee lifts off,
sure of wings, not feet.

LIGHT DAWNING

If only the plum-tree's dead leaves
first glanced
weren't seen as blue-tits back-lit.

DEAD SET

Stoat in pursuit
darts under the turning chain-wheel,
unscathed. Bike crashes.

CROSS–PURPOSES

Cat wavers walking the trellis top.
Sure sparrows
dart through its lattices.

MUD

Glum ducklings trudge
the mud shallows for yards.
The mother duck flies over.

SEASONAL DITHER

Late butterflies
fluttering around the shrubs
like early falling leaves.

RAIN-SPOTTING

The rain-filled plant tubs.
Four marksmen score
the four bulls repeatedly.

SIDE-LIGHT

Storm passed, the road gutter,
low lit, is leaded diamond
panes of water.

LIKELY TALES

BALLAD OF THE UNREPENTANT THIEF

A nice one, man, nice one.
   You'll not be soon forgotten:
'Mother, behold your son!'
   You're silk to my old cotton.
   The stuff I've done is rotten
But nothing like you've done.
   Your cunning is spot on.
God knows what you've begun.

And 'Son, behold your mother!'
   That was a master stroke.
How they'll hamstring each other,
   Poor lady, lumbered bloke,
   Fettered until they croak.
I hand it to you, brother,
   I tell you it's no joke.
Two people there you'll smother.

But that king crap won't wash.
    Real kings are just a number,
Just better wrapped worm nosh.
    This Jewish gink's just lumber
    The Romans leave to slumber.
All titles are so much tosh.
    And David's – bummed by mumblers
Of psalms and Torah bosh.

'You'll be in Paradise
    Today with me.' That twist
Another duff device.
    A hanged recidivist,
    He's no memorialist.
He pays the going price,
    Dying, nailed – foot and wrist.
He won't cop for life twice.

'Forsaken!' Well, dead right.
    The Old Man always scoots,
The usual fly-by-night;
    He never gives two hoots.
    What d'you expect from brutes?
But don't think it's pure spite.
    Mutt's terrified of roots,
Usually skint and tight.

'It's finished!' That's the key.
    You've got it in the bag.
The world'll not break free
    Of that tacky little tag;
    Good as that other brag:
No man remember me!
    The not-to-mention gag.
Remembered that'll be

Yet there I have the edge:
    Forgotten's for the best,
Buried in cave, or cledge,
    Unmarked, uncited, blest.
    A lasting name's a pest,
Invoked like a snide pledge
    To stop the living rest.
It's guilt dusting a ledge.

SPRAT TO CATCH A MACKEREL

King Mark was trying to train the wayward Prince
who'd skipped the chores of Maundy and Good Friday.
If he could see him now, he'd turn from puce
to raddled face. His son would think it delightful
as he dozed there, catching flies beneath the trees,
rocked gently by the flow in a purloined rum-tum.

But flies, he thought, small fish. Could his rum-tum
be used to catch a sprat or mackerel? The Prince
found metaphor and angle quite delightful,
picturing his father togged up tight for Friday,
hot and bothered, turning from raddled to puce
while he lazed, cool and carefree under green trees.

The King was sick to death of family trees.
'Oh, sprat to catch a mackerel in a rum-tum,'
he summoned Alice Fitzjohn, turning puce,
a shapely lass to catch his wayward Prince.
He'd show him off on Easter Day, not Friday,
his triumph would be more than most delightful.

Miss Alice Fitzjohn looked her best, delightful,
her minimal bikini, fetching puce,
as she manoeuvred the royal launch past trees.
she was determined she would catch the Prince,
sprawled unsuspecting in his stolen rum-tum.
she'd hook the idling whopper, her Man Friday.

This was certainly an excellent Good Friday.
She spotted a Princely leg she thought delightful.
so there he was, the handsome, wayward Prince.
She closed in, grabbed the painter of the rum-tum
and towed it off at speed beyond the trees,
and here was she in scanty, fetching puce.

The Prince, wet-legged, climbed in, a trifle puce.
'I'm not up to Good Friday. I've a rum tum.
Let's go back to my hideout in the trees,'
he said, undoing the bikini's tie, delightful.
'Hands off, your Highness, off; you're my man Friday.
you've come aboard. And now abroad, my Prince.

'It's ours, this Good Friday. We're exiles, Prince,
in transports of delight. Ditch phone. Chuck puce.
Cut loose from purloined rum-tum, family trees.'

THE DOWSER
>For Marjorie and John Bowers

A dowser working on the moor
zigzagged across a course and back.
When asked what he was searching for:
some special lode in rift, or crack.
>Geologists? They had no luck.
>Retired, pride hurt, and passed the buck.

It stopped at me and here I am.
I'll find a vein. *Who needs this stuff?*
Most companies think dowsing's a scam.
I'll find the mineral, proof enough
>that dowsers have their expertise.
>Besides we charge much cheaper fees.

Few firms would risk their name and fate
employing your occult sleight of hand.
True. That's why I'm a secret of state.
Today I'll make you understand.
>Assist me in the donkey work
>and I'll teach you dowsing, company perk.

Right. Then you take these coloured sticks
and place them where I say they go.
I'll say which colour where to fix,
a working record of what we'll know.

Okay. Work first, then training how.
It's back to searching. Watch me now.
        * * *

What were we looking for and why?
I told you before: it's a secret of state.
The Admiralty needs to resupply
with a mineral vital to create
    essential naval camouflage.
    Their worked-out sources were never large.

How do the rods detect your target?
The answer is they don't. You do.
They'll merely show you where you marked it
with some preconscious reflex. One view
    is it picks up change in geomagnetic gradients;
    another's that they're sound-wave radiants.

The sundial shows the course of the sun.
The dial's passive the user reads.
Likewise the rods show where things run:
the body's reflex the dowser heeds.
    Why can't I trace what you could track?
    Water's easiest to learn you have the knack.

So don't you call it occult. My way
makes sense even if boffins don't know
which electro-magnetic wave-lengths sway
the dowser's rods and hands to show
    where he's received a dowse-response.
    Experience finds him what the client wants.

Beware the plague of obscurantist dowsers
who'll say it works in mystic ways.
They're half-baked pseudo-science browsers
who think it's done by cosmic rays,
    Psi, quantum physics, or spirit link
    in various shades of sky-blue pink.

Enough from me. Your turn to talk.
You show more interest than most I meet.
What do you do beside just walk?
My walk in life treads on other feet,
    with sharp eye, open, curious mind
    and pocket note-book, best unlined.

So I observe but what do you do
or is it also a secret of state?
I'm a dodgy type as I thought you.
Poets aren't thought to carry weight.
    As dowsers are, we're judged outlandish
    with brain-waves, and you with rods you brandish.

A note-book's safer. Your rods you aim,
you jaywalked zigzag along a line.
It seemed our work was much the same
in ways it's tricky to define.
    Artists take a line for a walk.
    The donné line's what poets stalk.

Like dowsing? That seems a bit farfetched.
Right. Metaphors: my pen walks a sheet,
hand seeking a poem to be sketched.
When found, experience walks the beat.
    The eye and mind find idea, word,
    rhythms the inner ear has heard.

The general public feels scant need
for poets, and given what some write,
I sympathise and must concede.
But some of us bring depths to light.
    Right. You're also a dowser now.
    Thanks to you. Poems? Don't ask how.

I'll not be versing dowsing. Sorry.
Poets are reckoned mad enough
already. – We hardly found a quarry
to stake out for your mineral stuff.
    True. It's a start and you or we
    will find some more. *Is there a fee?*

ENVOI

THE RODS: CLOSURE AND DISCLOSURE
For John Bowers

Jammed by electronic chaos, and all that jazz,
the mind's attentiveness is overlaid.
The earth has waves and noises as water has
But now we're deaf without external aid.
Yet still the earth and waters may be heard
bodily when our senses are unblurred.

The rods locate the waters underground;
reveal the shuffled dead, their broken bones
and relics ploughed ages through from pit and mound;
detect blind springs nearby the ancient stones
that circle standing waves the seasons tune,
varying with tide and storm, the sun and moon.

Not magic, nor etheric spirits: flesh and blood,
whose subliminal wits progress has over-ridden,
the human sympathy with earth and flood.
Bodily wisdom moves the rods unbidden
at standing waves, blind springs. The megaliths
resound to sun, moon, earth, not guesswork myths.

ABOUT THE AUTHOR

PETER DALE

Poet and verse translator Peter Dale's work has been well received in literary quarters. His most recent books are: *Diffractions: New and Collected Poems,* and *Local Habitation*. His most reprinted translations are *Selected Poems of François Villon* and Dante's Divine Comedy in terza rima. All of his books are published by Anvil Press Poetry Limited, London. www.anvilpresspoetry.com
He can be heard reading his poems on a National Poetry Archive CD: ISSBN 1 905556 12 8

R. V. Bailey has written of Peter Dale's poems:

Musical, measured, his work appears deceptively casual – conversational even. But it is scrupulously crafted, the writing of an experienced and able practitioner, alert to the cadences of everyday speech as well as to the echoes of myth and poetic heritage. His poetic skill is unobtrusive, played down, a matter of echo and hint; it has a sure-footedness that's most delicate.